This book is for you if...

- You are searching for answers

- You are looking for wisdom and clarity

- You want to understand the truth about your life

- You are looking for inspiration and direction

This book, written by healer and wise, dedicated yogi, Damaris Lau, is the result of many years' insight that has led several people home to themselves. This is the book that speaks directly to your heart!

"The Road Home – The Book That Speaks To You" is written in a loving and poetic language and can not avoid giving food for thoughts and reflection. The book embraces and releases numerous big questions and problems of life – in few words and with great compassion.

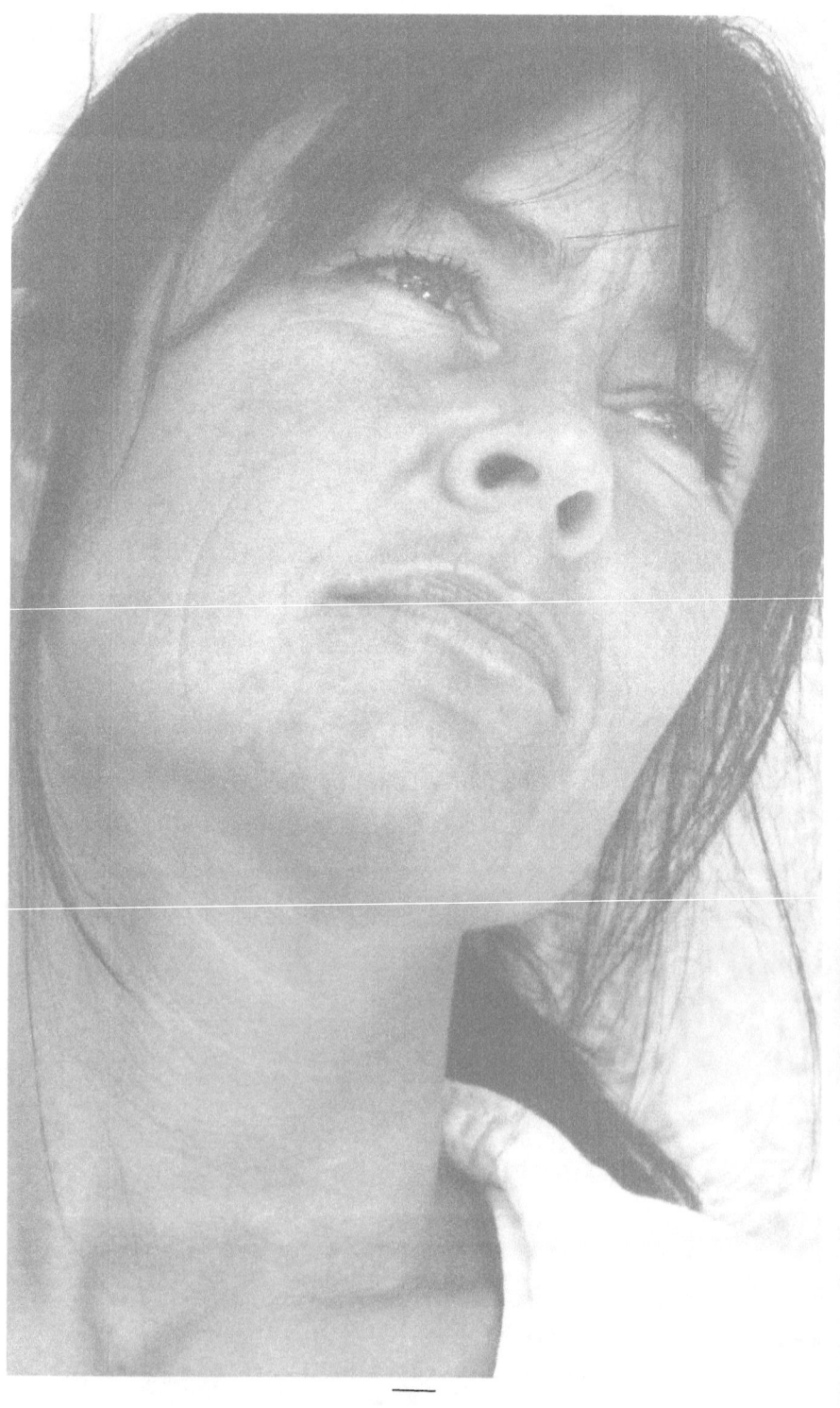

Damaris Lau

Damaris Lau (born 1969), lives on Bornholm in Denmark. Over many years she has helped thousands of people all over the world, using her clairvoyant and healing abilities. All kinds of people seek Damaris' help, and the results, plus the great gratitude, speak for themselves. Damaris helps people put words to their feelings and cures their illnesses – through talking, counselling and healing.

Today Damaris has devoted her life to help people find "The road home" by showing them among other things, ways to liberation through mind training, meditation, the special breathing techniques of Pranayama, her own special, deep and releasing Shiva-yoga, mantra and prayer. Every day she also receives people who are ill, or have questions about life and seek spiritual counselling.

With her knowledge and love, she helps people to obtain a better life, and teaches them to free themselves from their minds and the noise that is around them and in them. She also teaches them the importance of forgiveness, to show compassion and to be able to free yourself from the past, which is already non-existent.

She holds a sincere desire to promote all the beauty that exists in every creature and every soul. And that everyone can learn and evolve in life, spiritually and as a human being, regardless of their past, and from what they have come from. Damaris embraces everyone who wants to follow the path.

Every month Damaris receives numerous confidential letters from various people, who ask her to bless them and take their concerns/prayers within her prayers. The letters contain everything from wishes of freedom from diseases, about jobs, sorrow, loneliness, love, spiritual enlightenment, clarity, best wishes for sick loved ones, parents' wishes for their children, and everything that stirs in human life. She does not read all letters, but they are all taken within her prayer.

Damaris herself is not linked to a religion, but her innate wisdom rests, among other things, in Buddha's spirit, and her love emanates from her ever-faithful trust in Christ. She therefore believes that you do not need to seek refuge, or in any way be religious or a believer to come and receive insights, teachings and blessings from her. Damaris therefore embraces anyone who seeks, and believe herself that all living beings should have the opportunity to achieve and live in eternal bliss and freedom.

Her wish for all souls is that they will have the possibility to seek refuge through prayer, mantra and meditation, as well as a better and easier access to the wise, educational, sacred scriptures, which have been written as a help and guide in life for all living beings who seek the path, whether they are believers or not, or if they have devoted their life to a particular guru, God or not.

Damaris believes that we as human beings can neither judge or allow ourselves to stand in the way of others who would like to search for, learn, or otherwise wish to have spiritual enlightenment.

As she always says: the Divine/Love embraces everyone, without demands or reservations, but always and unconditionally!

In 2012 Damaris built an ashram in the middle of the beautiful countryside outside of Rønne on Bornholm. From here she bestows her many teachings, hosts retreats and also teaches her yoga etc. In addition, she organizes sessions with prayer, mantra and blessings for all.

You can seek shelter from the daily life for a while and use the beautiful space for free, for prayer, mantra, meditation, simply silence or something else. The ashram is today very well attended.

Damaris does not want too much attention because she believes it is not her who is of interest, but all the souls who attends the daily consultations and her teachings/lectures since everything they do, all that they are, and the whole of their development, is far more important and bigger.

If you ask Damaris Lau what she is, she replies with a twinkle in her eye: just the same as you are - passing through.

Thank you

I wish to express heartfelt gratitude to my beloved son who through the years has shown immense understanding, respect and compassion for the time my calling has demanded.
Thank you for being my son, for the person you are and for the wonder of being your mother. Your beautiful heart, and the great insight you possess, have graced my life's journey.

It is with deep gratitude that I express my thanks to all the people who have been a part of my life, and those who still are. Without you I would not be who I am today.
Thank you for the many hours devoted to editing and proof-reading, as well as the vast amount of patience it has required in doing so. Without you and the abundance of love and understanding shown for my being, this book would not have come into existence.
From my heart thanks to my son's grandmother, for many hours given to translating this book into English. Thank you for your love and understanding.
From my innermost, thanks to my always faithful and outstanding assistant and manager, Sussi Rømer Rasmussen. Thank you for gathering and translating this book further with your compassion and loving approach. Thanks for always being faithful in your tasks.
Thank you for becoming my manager and for the amazing cooperation we have both through dharma work and everything new that awaits us.

Everything for the joy and happiness for all living creatures. Always will you have my trust... Thank you.

Thank you to all the souls who have put aside their journeys in some way, shape or form, to seek my help and advice. What a joy and honour it has been and still is, to be allowed to help those of you who need counselling and aid; it goes without saying that it has been an influential factor in the birth of this book. Thank you.

Thank you to those who have brokered the right contacts in order to pave the way for this book, and for having supported its message.

Thanks to the publishers for believing in me and accepting my book; for the energy poured into this book, and to all of those who have been a part of it.

To the graphic designers who so beautifully understood how to realize my dream – I thank you!

Thank you to those who have been a constant source of support when things were going against me, and thank you for embracing me as I am.

Thank you for the realisation of this book.

☙

The Road Home

The book that speaks directly to you

Damaris Lau

Published by
Filament Publishing Ltd
14, Croydon Road, Beddington,
Croydon, Surrey CR0 4PA
Telephone: +44 (0)20 8688 2598
www.filamentpublishing.com

The Road Home by Damaris Lau
© 2019 Damaris Lau

The right of Damaris Lau to be identified as the Author of the Work has been asserted by her in accordance wih the Copyright, Designs and Patents Act 1988.

All rights reserved. The book may not be copied in anyway without the prior written permission of the publishers.

ISBN 978-1-912256-61-7
Printed by IngramSpark

Photo credit: Berit Hvassum
(Mala and Damaris portrait on the back)
Kristina Wulff (Damaris and horse)
Translator: Sussi Rømer Rasmussen

Contents

Dear Reader	14
We human beings	17
~We are all different	18
~Remembering love	20
~Living the "right" kind of life	22
~Feeling insufficient	27
~Seeking help	29
~To walk your own way	31
~To judge others	33
~To make choices	36
~To face the unknown	39
~Self reflection	40
~To forgive	43
~Being busy	44

~The family	46
~The universal love	50
The truth	52
The mind	55
Daring to set foot on new paths	59
Find your path in life	62
To offer help and let go afterwards	65
The trials of life	67
Decisions	71
Patience	73
Dear divinity	82
Be true to your feelings	86
Self-knowledge	91
What you send out	96
Anger	99
Anxiety	103

Suffering and pain	106
To escape	112
Loneliness	114
Being together in life	119
Friendship	125
When two people separate	128
Death and sorrow	135
To forgive yourself	138
Love	140
Injustice	144
Forgiveness	147
To be present	151
Which faith is the real one?	153
Who is God?	156
Who can pray?	158
My prayer	163

Dear reader

This book is not the truth of all truths, but my truth, which from the bottom of my heart I wish to share with those of you who are searching. Through many years, it has been my desire to write a book, but I felt I lacked the ability to do so. There is a big difference between verbally expressing yourself as opposed expressing yourself in the written form.

My inner most wish is to be allowed to pass on what I have experienced, the blessings I have received and to share what life has shown and given to me.

I am extremely humble towards all the beauty and divinity having filled my life. And I feel the deepest respect for all the insights I have been given.

Therefore, it is of great importance for me, to tell everyone reading this book that, in no way, am I the one to be honoured for the words of wisdom and love it contains – I am just the one passing it on!

My intention is to help those people seeking consolation and insight in their lives. To be able to bring light and love, as well as show them some of the wonders life has to offer.

To help people see the possibilities in life, and to set those on course who seek a way to embrace humanity with love.

I believe that all of us can be part of making a difference, and I believe that the Universe of God embraces all souls.

To me, it is a great honour and a bliss to be allowed to give birth to this book.

May all who read this book feel loved and appreciated; may you feel that life is worth living and may you achieve enlightenment in your heart.

May you find your way home…

We human beings

*I see the light of my heart, there on the candlestick.
I follow it gratefully and with deep respect and
humility, knowing
that the wick counts my steps in the days of life.*

*Truly I know deep inside,
that my inner flame needs my care and nurture
as the soul of my flame is my call of responsibility
and therefore can not be cared for or owned by others.*

*The flame is burning softly, and I shield my life,
from coldness and human winds,
knowing by heart,
that thus my light burns the best.*

*In time my light will dwindle, and my wick's days
will be numbered.
Deep within my soul I know
that my life as God's flame,
soon shall burn elsewhere in spirit.
Softly, with my last breath, I let go.
The light of a new soul,
can now take my earthly place on the candlestick.*

It can be difficult to be a human being in the world we live in, based on what we are, what we want to be, and not least what we would like to develop into. We begin as small, innocent, fragile souls, dependent on our parents, taking part in their lives and framework, created from choices that they once made.

~ We are all different

Early in our lives we have to take into consideration what life is offering us.
Most of us start by learning in school about the many academic branches we can use later on as communication with the outer world, whether be it in relation to a job or in our contact with people surrounding us.
Some are good at academic pursuits, and find it very easy to manage in this field. While others are not at all good at finding any coherence in academic subjects, and have to suffer all the years through school, feeling they have no value as a human being because they find that practical work and creativity as well as inner qualities, comes more naturally to them.
Time and time again they get the feeling of failure as they can not live up to the "common" norm of obtaining the required marks, being, sensitive creatures who think differently, who can not cope with the pressure of being in a world that demands high speed, modern lifestyle and above all, money, power and prestige. A world that has no room for, or time to listen to the feelings of others or to those of one's own. But no matter

who we are, or where we are, or from which circumstances we have sprung, we are all made of the same substance – only put together differently.
Meaning that our resources are given individually: some are fantastic at handling practical work, various crafts, and others good at art, or philosophical ideas.
There are also those whose strength it is to feel for others and see to their needs, which is an incredible help and support in a more social context – they may therefore be perfect to function among human beings who need some kind of social, physical or psychological guidance.
Others find their strength in handling pure academic knowledge, and are therefore clever at solving more administrative tasks, which is also a very important part of our society.
One branch is no more right than another as they all extend from the same root.
For that reason it is important that we as human beings try our best to help, and give room to others and to ourselves, so that we may individually find our strengths and nurture them, and give them the necessary space and time to develop in the best way, from what we are.
We are all on our way in life, and we all want to pursue to live a good life and maybe a better life, than the one we are living right now.
Many souls have been inspired by the thought of something they might wish to try in life, maybe something from their innermost being that they have long wished to act upon.

Unfortunately, it often only remains just a thought in the mind. To be able to change our lives and the way we live it, we are forced to stop and ask ourselves the following questions:

who am I?
where am I?
where am I going?

~ Remembering love

I have deliberately not yet mentioned the word that makes all the difference in our lives, and the world we live in; namely the word love.
You might think that I had forgotten the most essential of all by not mentioning it, but no! How could I ever fail to mention this amazing, beautiful and pivotal word, which is the entire basis of empathy, compassion, forgiveness and insight, and the only way to reunite human kind on this common planet.
The only way to become whole, and thereby constituting a unity among what is half - yet love is what we have forgotten, we have forgotten ourselves, the others, and the fact that love is the most important basic ingredient in all that we, as human beings, take part in.

We have each been given this life, with free will as part of the package, and each of us has been granted a mouthpiece that speaks from our hearts, and which always will answer the questions we pose in life and to ourselves, if we dare to ask!

The art is not to just keep this voice in our hearts, but to listen to it, and have the courage to stand by it and take action.

Many a fight has been fought, and many fights are still fought by humans, but for what?
What is it we as human beings are continuously fighting for and against?
And who are we fighting against?
In the end, it is ourselves we are fighting as we have ceased to listen to the universal pulse that beats with our heartbeats.

Think of all the time we spend fighting in our attempt to obtain what should be the norm of a good life; but what is a good life?
And if we did not fight what would our time then be spent on?
Love?
We are all different pieces in this world's huge puzzle, but not all of us fit in where with anticipation, we were placed.
No matter how hard we try to turn and twist ourselves as a piece in a puzzle, and no matter how hard we use violence and power to try force ourselves into a place that somebody else might have fitted better into, it will just cause the picture to crack, as the frame will be bend, and the picture will break up.
If we are to make this puzzle complete, we have to individually figure out what we are, and where we can be placed; in this way our soul's lustre will not break nor crack.
But it is not always easy trying to figure out who we really are,

and how and where we find ourselves in this busy and, at times, insensitive and unfeeling world.

It requires time, quiet space, inner reflection and most important of all, our heartfelt wish. To change our lives and the way we live it, we have to adjust and prepare ourselves to the fact that every decision has a consequence.

~ Living the "right" kind of life

In many cases it is a question of daring to let go of control and regulations. This is one of the most vulnerable points – daring to let go of the safe framework of our daily life, and daring to break the norm for the "right" kind of life.

But what is the right kind of life?

Is it what we watch on television and what we read about?

Or is it the way others live their lives?

There is nothing wrong with the lives we watch on television or see around us, but there is if we let ourselves be influenced and controlled by our surroundings, as you can not say that one life is more "right" than another. However, it is certain that love makes all the difference in every life, regardless.

Therefore, I ask you these questions:

- Is there enough time for the most essential in your life?

- When was the last time you enjoyed taking a day off, devoting yourself to what you love the most ?

-When did you allow yourself to enjoy a wonderful meal, where you could taste that it was made with a loving hand?

- When did you last tell your loved one that you love him or her?

- When did you spend time with the people you deeply care about?

- When have you asked yourself whether you are satisfied with yourself, and whether there is anything you, as a human being, perhaps could become better at?

- When have you listened to the music of nature, of trees swaying in the wind, leaves rustling in their treetops, looked at the ocean and enjoyed the sight of the peaceful motion of the waves, laid on your back in a meadow, just gazing at a blue sky while swallows sang and the breeze of a light, warm wind caressed you?

- When have you thought about your heart's inner feeling, and felt its beat, beating for your life?

- When have you called your life into account?

- When have you asked yourself: is this my life as I wish to live it?

There is nothing wrong with striving after and improving a

career, but there is in the way it might occupy space in your life.

Many people suffer from constant stress and inner fear of not being able to keep up with changes in their work field.
The more they show that they can handle the job of two people, the more people are let go, and then in turn the more work is put on the one left alone in the post.
More and more illnesses plague our lives while the necessary time for healing is reduced.
Fear of losing money to pay for the life we have built overshadows the self-knowledge that a heart in distress requires peace and quiet to regain its natural rhythm, in order to heal body, mind and soul.
At the loss of dear and near ones, grief is not allotted the necessary time to heal, as time at work, handling practical tasks and internal pressure, rob human beings of the time they so deeply need, in the form of peace and quiet, to be able to get through a difficult time.
The more materialism, the more work, and the less time for yourself.
What is the use of aiming for a big and beautiful home if you have no time to enjoy it?

As is often the case, we human beings do not stop until it is too late, despite the signals that our body and soul, over a longer period of time, have been trying to send. That there is something we need to pay attention to, something is not as it is supposed to be - a painful cry from your inner of body and soul.

To begin with it may occur as small signs, like fatigue and anger as a result of internal and external pressure, followed by a lot of other signs.
It is by not listening to the early signals that we may let more serious diseases develop as our immune system breaks down since it does not get the time to fully heal before we again expose it to further pressure. Eventually, every human function will burst and we will collapse either internally or externally.

It is not guaranteed that we will be happy when we finally reach the top. We may have set that as a goal for ourselves but we might discover that we have been climbing the wrong mountain all along, and that it was a waste of effort and energy.
Even though we may be successful in our work and have achieved good results, it does not mean that it was what we had intended to do in life. We are often forced painfully to confront ourselves before realizing that it was not what we wanted in life, nor were we aware of the consequences when we started.

Now and then we make choices in our life that we regret, and we feel it as a big defeat, having to admit to ourselves and to those around us that we have made a mistake in our choice. However, the strength is exactly to reach the realisation that things not worked out as expected, and then having the courage to stop and find a new path.
This is not a failure, but an insight in the teachings that sometimes it is necessary to walk the "wrong" path, in order to

see the "better" and "right" path.

Those without a job, feeling they have nothing to get up for in the morning, may suffer in their lack of involvement in life and society.
Equally, those at the top of society, who spend 95 % of their time on their job, also suffer as they miss the time to feel life.
Both have the opportunity for a better life, if they truly wish it and dare to take it.
We human beings have created a world where the very waves we ride on may be the one drowning us in the end.
We let ourselves drown due to the lack of life's oxygen of love, and no longer see the essentials that give life and nourishment to every human soul.

We are surrounded by constant noise from machines, and are often interrupted by messages from devices that make us stop our chores, to consider the various requests..
We have become accustomed to this noise, thereby creating an unnatural need to constantly stimulate the eye, the ear or the brain.
The most essential and important has been forgotten, namely the stimulation of our inner soul and heart which are starved of the kind of nourishment derived from peace, love, care and human sincerity.

At times humans may even become anxious when everything becomes quiet, or just stops for a moment because it has forgotten that every flower grows the best when the wind does not tear into it since when it is constantly moved around, it will not manage to take root on firm ground.

~ Feeling insufficient

Many people feel lost in this world, and let their life be overshadowed by feelings of insufficiency as well as the lack of ability to be part of society, because their unconventional way of thinking or sensitivity makes it hard for them to comply with what others consider normal. Rejection in the job market or in social circles may result in much mental suffering which, in worst cases, may develop into physical illnesses. They fall behind in the system and end up hiding behind a wall of loneliness, disease and excuses, which are then used to prevent themselves from participating in life or working in a job that they can not live up to because of human or spiritual reasons. These people are often characterized as 'losers' in society. In reality, they are just fragile, sensitive souls, who find it very difficult to naturally fit into the society in which we live in. They are what I prefer to call 'souls of light'; they can not tolerate too much wind before their flame of light becomes unsteady, but they are enriched with a strength and an ability to give light elsewhere, if they are just allowed to be where the wind is gentle and where there is a different approach to life.
They struggle through school where they experience one failure after another, they lose self-confidence and feel "stupid" as they

do not understand numbers and writing. Often, they are also limited or incapable of social interaction with their peers, or they are not around them, and must stand alone on the sidelines while experiencing being left further and further behind as there is no place for their kind.

Nothing is wrong with these souls, they are merely misunderstood because their abilities and talents lies elsewhere, via practical functions. What sufferings they must go through, and what humiliations they have to put up with, being stamped as "inadequate"! But inadequate for what?

Well, inadequate for what other people think is a "real" life and a "real" human being, a life and a human being moulded in certain boxes and frameworks.

But to those of you who feel that you do not fit in, I would just like to say that there is a life for you, therefore you have to hold on to your belief and hope, and seek it when you are ready. God has a plan for all of us, it is just a question of figuring out yours. This means that as a human being you have to relate to who you are at the core of your being, and that you do not need to, and must not, change what you were meant to be from the beginning, but learn to live with it, in relation to yourself and the people around you. Regardless which position we humans occupy, there is always a way forward, in one way or another, if we dare to just take the first step.

God has not placed us in this world to be lost, but to allow each and everyone of us the opportunity to partake in this world, based on who we are inside.

~ Seeking help

It is understandable that more and more people seek help from a physician or from the alternative/spiritual world, whether it be for assistance with physical health or the mind.
This is due to the fact that we often are well aware that our life is not how it is supposed to be, yet we continue on with it as the familiarity gives us a sense of security.
Currently, there are numerous ways concerning how we as human beings can obtain insight into ourselves and our lives, and really there is no way of saying that one treatment is better than another, if only it assists the individual person in gaining a better, healthier and richer life.
We must not forget to gain insight into our own feelings, not only in relation to those around us, but also in relation to ourselves and our own attitude towards life. I can easily understand that it is difficult having to choose a form that fits the individual person.
It is of great importance that we condemn neither scientific assistance, nor the alternative, as both have the purpose of helping people.
All is part of everything, as all emanates from the same.

You may as a human being discover essential values in seeking the answer of truth in life as it provides a direction to go in, a cornerstone as an anchorage.
However, it is important to understand that you do not become

a lesser person just because you do not believe in something. Whether you seek answers in spirituality or try to seek answers in nature, or somewhere else entirely, it is not what is crucial for a better life.

The person seeking a better life will achieve it when they learn to act from kindness of a pure heart in a healthy body and soul. There is not just one, but many paths - the key is to find your own way of searching from inside yourself.

As mentioned, we all come from different backgrounds, and we are all different in our attitude to life, but even though there are many paths and ways, there only exists one certain way of achieving life's wisdom and insight, and that is through the heart's inner truths. This is where our transformation takes place, and this is where the battle must be fought.

As human we are extremely afraid of pain and the unknown, and when we choose to walk down new paths, in order to reach new heights and widths to obtain insight, we put ourselves at risk of experiencing pain or rejection by the very people we previously thought were close to us.

But whatever kind of suffering or pressure you are subject to, remember that if that is the cost of reaching the insight in yourself or into something bigger, then you will not be ordered to carry burdens bigger than you can bear.

The question is merely do you have the courage and will to dare.

The very moment you decide to seek something else, or to tread new paths in your life, then you have taken the first step.

~ To walk your own way

It is therefore of great importance that we do not force either ourselves or others down paths where we feel resistance, as this may suffocate any desire to improve as a human being, thus hamper a healthy soul in obtaining a good and better life.
We need to give each other room to be the person we are, and what we were created to be, all of us being of great value and serving our own purpose of being here; we each just need to find it in our own individual way.

The farmer, working in his yard and walking on his lush fields, is just as important as the top politician working on worldwide economic plans.
He who understands worldwide economics may not know nature's signs for a good harvest, just as the farmer may not know about economic speculations on a worldwide level; however, each has a unique knowledge within their area of expertise.

The same applies to those with an excellent education who have studied for years to obtain proof of their knowledge, preferably with honours.
But the stay-at-home, uneducated mother or father's role is just as important, as he/she must have an overview of food, grocery shopping and cleaning as well as raising their children in a loving and wise manner, so they can be prepared for and

strengthened in life.

Their efforts are not printed on a written certificate, but in the future of their children.

Therefore, it is not a question of some people being more important than others, but that we all continuously strive to be better.

It is important to understand that we are all at different stages in our life, and that each stage is individual to each and every human soul.

Nevertheless, it seems that we in some way are shaped or moulded by the world's norm of how we as human beings are supposed and meant to be, otherwise those around us can not control where or who we are individually.

We must not let ourselves be disrupted on our individual journey, as the journey is what makes us wiser as humans, by each of us having to find the most suitable path for ourselves and make our own physical and emotional journey.

One path can not be said to be better than another; it is only by individual searching that we will find the path best suited for who we are.

So seek, and you will find, leave no stone unturned if you need to, climb every mountain you might have to, if that is what is necessary for you, in order to gain your path. Should others shake their heads at you, remember that they do not do so to hurt you, but because they do not know better themselves; for a long time they themselves might have felt an urge to do

something else in their lives, but have not dared to take the step into the unknown.
Without courage and with inner sadness because of a grey everyday life, they find it the easiest to shake their heads at the one that dared.

Instead of closing yourself off to unknown paths, being open and receptive can in itself be a positive and helpful experience. Perhaps you have you tried twenty different paths before finding the one you can use? Be delighted at the one true path, instead of regretting the nineteen that did not seem to be right. Maybe you would not have recognized the one and possibly most important path if it had not been for the other nineteen.

~ To judge others

Our life on earth and our daily activities involves meeting and mingling with other people. Truly it is sad to witness someone demeaning another person at a social gathering. Speaking behind someone's back, ridiculing or degrading someone is, unfortunately, something that takes place at workplaces, at gatherings or in everyday life. And we know very well that it is wrong to speak ill of another person, but it often happens because we do not give others the space to think and act differently from what we perhaps ourselves are used to.
The worst part is that the person who is the victim of slander and belittling is often not aware of what the problem is, or

what he or she has done. And how should the person in question be able to find out, and therefore get a chance to rectify the problem, if there is no kind soul to tell them?

I often think of the people I meet in town that stick out in some way, perhaps having come from an unfortunate background. I notice those around us keeping these souls at a distance. In reality, it is not because people do not like them, but because they may have been told a demeaning story about this poor soul, and from that, choose to judge.
Judging others is very prominent in our everyday life. We allow ourselves to be influenced by those around us and listen far too much to other people's opinions, letting them affect our minds and be carried away, while mercilessly judging, with lack of respect and love for the one who is vulnerable.
We do this, despite the fact that we as human beings have no right to allow ourselves to judge, as we do not know the whole truth, nor are we pure enough ourselves to make judgements.
We forget to look behind the façade, and perhaps do not see the human being collapsing in tears behind closed doors because those around them judge so harshly that everything seems impossible and without meaning, and in fact can deprive even the slightest hope from them.
Nor do we see the inside of this soul fighting for its very existence and calling; when it finally reaches its goal, it is only met with envy.
We must not forget that some of those who have made it to the top, also had to crawl there. And the ones crawling - well, one

of them might just be the one who saves you, by extending a helping hand from the top.

We all make mistakes in our actions as human beings, and often we regret them deeply and must each suffer the consequences. However, we must also be allowed to make mistakes as none of us can see ourselves as perfect and flawless. We must not let our mind feel joy when we watch a soul falling, being the same pain for him or her, as it was for us the times we had to fall.

It is better to make room, without condemning; so that each of us can walk freely without threat of oppression; that we all are permitted to walk the paths we need to; and that we all may be allowed to fall many times, if necessary. For the one that falls suffers enough pain as it is, and our task is not to inflict further pain on one that suffer the consequences of his act.

We need to be less affected by all that we hear and see, because in reality we can only allow ourselves to look at our own feet treading our own path.

It is not done with malice toward the world when we accidentally judge someone, but because we sometimes are weak as human beings. We allow ourselves to be dragged along with the current, and therefore do and say things we could have done differently and better, had we only bothered to take notice of how we ourselves would have felt, if others were judging us.

We need to give each other room for having the opportunity to improve, as it is through our mistakes that we learn to become better human beings. Everyone should be given a chance, as anyone may have need of one.

~ To make choices

Often we ignore that little voice speaking to our inner conscience, thus avoiding the painful truth for a while.
But it is inevitably that eventually in our life we will be confronted with the acknowledgement that we can not get around the talk of truth from our heart, and we therefore can not find peace until we realize and do something - if not now, then the next time!
And if it is not the next time around, it will be when we ourselves are ready and have the courage to do so.
We deeply want to become better, and to know the truth, whether it is about ourselves or those around us, but often we get so scared when we look truth in the eye that we dare not take the full step, fearing the uncertainty that follows. However, life functions in such a way that before we can venture onto unknown paths, we have to let go of our foothold on the old path and make sure we take that foot with us - otherwise it will never be a complete step, and no steps will therefore have been taken.
As human beings we have to be open to all that life has to offer. We do not need to go along with everything, but most importantly the times where we feel that it is necessary, for what we sincerely wish from the heart can show itself and be fulfilled.

As children, we have to stumble and fall many times before learning how to walk on our two feet; had we remained sitting, we would not be able to walk out into life.

Many people have in their upbringing been raised with the expectation to mould and conform themselves to those around them and respect the opinions and judgement of that environment. They quickly learn that if they give into and please those around them, they get acceptance. Or do they? The answer would be to seek inside ourselves, for an answer on what is right for us as human beings, as only we can determine and feel what is right or wrong for ourselves.
Far too often people make "mistakes" in their choices in life as they listen far too much to what other people think is best for them. The result is that we spend way too much time seeking outside ourselves, causing us to walk many detours in life, and suffer great pain and big defeats on our path in life.
It is not pleasant to disappoint our near ones with the choices we make, but the pain of disappointment is greater when we discover that we have compromised the choice of life that we wanted to lead.
It is possible that others may not comprehend the choices or re-selections we make, and it is possible that we might hurt or disappoint those we deeply care about - but we need to keep in mind that we do this, not to act against them, but because it is what feels right for ourselves, and because that is the truth of our heart's voice.

We may often feel that the people around us are the cause of our stagnation, and that it is those around us that limit our possibilities in life. But in fact, we are our own limitation – nobody can limit us, unless we allow them to.

Often, we let it become the cause, or the excuse, for not acting on the wishes we have for our life. In reality, it is often a question of our own fear of the unknown that makes us find an excuse for not treading new paths.
Although deep down we know what would be best for us, we have a tendency to focus on the obstacles rather than the opportunities - thereby, losing sight of our heart's interest and what it spoke of.

We forget the freedom given to us from birth, we forget the joy of being free to choose as long as we are ready to face the consequences of placing our lives into the hands of the universe, and allowing it to lead the way.

When you as a human being choose to seek deeper into yourself, or when you seek new paths and boundaries in life, you will often notice that the people around you change their behaviour toward you. But in reality it is not necessarily the people around you who change, but you yourself - because you are going through some sort of inner transformation.
This makes you act and react differently from how you did before, which people around you will then start to notice. Keep in mind that they relate to you as you 'used' to be, and

how could they do otherwise, when that is what they are accustomed to?

~To face the unknown

We seem to feel at ease when things are familiar, and it may be incredibly difficult having to face the new unknown.
We do not intend to harm those around us when we are not always forthcoming toward the unknown; we act this way because we are insecure, and do not know how to handle the situation.
This is one of the explanations to often, why we do not have the courage to ask about each other, or vice versa, why we do not dare to give sincere answers, in our fear of how those around us will react.
As human beings we may even be taken by surprise when a kind soul suddenly asks sincere questions about our well being, or wants our opinion on something.
We are not accustomed to anyone showing compassion or interest in us as a person, and may react awkwardly, both emotionally and verbally.
In many circumstances we choose, in our evasion, to say that we are fine – despite the contrary that something is troubling our heart, and we really needed to talk to somebody about it. Instead we get deadlocked and avoid the truth, a truth that reveals ourselves and may expose our personality.
Often it happens because we do not want to be a burden to anyone, nor do we want to be different, therefore we would

rather bear the truth in our inner self, hidden and silent.
All this due to the fear of those around us not accepting us for what we are or believe in – the fear of being ridiculed or exposed as being different.

The more we try to escape ourselves, the more awkward our relationships become with each other, life and ourselves. We are all different from each other as we are different on the inside of our soul.

It is much easier to tell the truth as it is, and each explain how we feel it in our hearts, as we rarely feel alike, nor are we alike. We human beings need to get better at handling the truth with respect for each other's differences, and the lives we lead and carry out, not least out of respect to ourselves. What a wonderful and liberating experience it is when a human being dares to break the norm, and ask sincere questions to another soul. What a gift they might have been given that day! A person who showed true interest and who was open and receptive to questions. Someone who did so without thinking a lot of thoughts first, but merely did it straight from the heart.
We forget to take the time to ask about each other's well being, forget to dare to show compassion and care out of fear of doing or saying something wrong.

~ Self reflection

We have created a world where we do not always place proper

value on the life that has been given to us.

We forget that it is not necessary to struggle with each other, but rather give room, so there is space for each and everyone. It would be so much easier to give room to each other's ways of being because when we put up resistance towards what is different than what we are used to, it is a negative energy we give birth to.

The easiest is to blame others for what we were not successful at! But we each have to realize that other people are not always to blame for our own unhappiness or the hardships of our lives.

This is where I feel that it is important to take a good hard look at ourselves, and hold ourselves accountable for why we are in this particular situation, or why our life is the way it is.

At times we may come to the realization that similar situations have occurred earlier in our lives, just in another way.

Instead of feeling a victim of those around us and other people we encounter, it would be a great strength to understand that being a victim is only possible if we accept being one ourselves. Through soul-searching we will come to discover sides of our personality which we have to acknowledge can be improved or changed. Often it is the smallest change in the way we behave that makes the biggest difference, whether it is in relation to ourselves or others. We often tend to ignore the side of ourselves that we dislike as it is unpleasant, being confronted with the darker sides of our own ego.

You may be tempted to believe that it is those around you who have to change before you yourself can feel better, but indeed it is only us who can make the decisions, and only us who each have to take the consequence of, and the responsibility for, the choices we make. It is only ourselves who must walk those heavy, and at times painful, but vital steps in our lives before we experience the transformation in our inner self.

We stand in our lives where our choices have placed us.

The road to self-knowledge can be very painful, and it demands that we sincerely want it, not just in words, but by searching our heart and then putting it into action.

What a prison we put ourselves in when we maintain not wanting, nor daring to acknowledge our own flaws and shortcomings.

What limitations we impose on ourselves, and at times those around us.

What happiness it is to feel the relief triggered when you acknowledge the mistakes you have made, as it opens the door to joy and light in your existence.

Then we no longer have to spend vast amounts of energy on keeping ourselves stuck in fixed frames of opinions and attitudes, but instead begin to see what has been hiding behind closed doors that we did not believe possible for ourselves.

A possible new side of life and the universe will appear only when we open doors that before seemed closed.

When one door closes, another will open

It is by being open and receptive that we encounter joy and recognize the essentials as there are no longer any limitations, but instead, possibilities that present themselves. This creates an inner sense of satisfaction making it so much easier to love our fellow man, as it is by inner pleasure that we are open and free, and able to receive and give.

We no longer have to feel inferior, for now we have cleared the inner chamber of our conscience and formerly dark mind. The more we allow ourselves to be filled with the positive things that life has to offer, the more we have to give and the more we can receive.

A previous shortage of life-affirming joy and energy will be replaced in many cases with an excess when we accept what we are, and what we can improve in our inner self-knowledge.

~ To forgive

After a process of self-knowledge, we reach forgiveness.
The forgiveness of others and ourselves.
This may be one of the most difficult tasks to handle because we are human beings.
To be able to forgive oneself for the mistakes one made towards others can be very painful as it may be incredibly hard to give into, and let go of, the destructive thoughts being awakened in that moment when, with great regret and

powerlessness, we feel and realize what we have done.
We must keep in mind that we are human, and that we make mistakes, not out of evil, but because we do not know better. We can not change our past, but we can learn from it and apply those lessons to our future. Likewise, it seems difficult to forgive our fellow human beings, however, it is important to remember the freedom we grant another human being, not least ourselves, when we forgive others for the wrongs they might have done in their powerlessness.
Imagine how different our daily life would be, and how different our world would be, if we each could learn to become better at forgiveness – what a burden the world would be relieved of.

~ Being busy

So many thoughts wander in our minds, thoughts of what we would like to change in our daily life or in life in general. Thoughts of everything we would like to obtain, and all that we have not yet obtained.

Often we impose a burden on ourselves, blaming ourselves as human beings because we do not feel that we are able to keep up.
Perhaps we attempt to make more time for leisure, but what is the point of more leisure when we often choose to spend it, on previous neglected matters that we have not had time for

beforehand - and it can be very difficult figuring out where to begin, and what the most important thing to begin with is.

We so desperately want to be in control of everything, and the last thing we want, is to disappoint our near and dear ones. In our heart, we wish to make everyone happy, and only thereby are we able to feel satisfaction in ourselves. However, it is important that if there are things we want to change, we must proceed with one task at a time, beginning with the easiest and completing it and try to stay focused while we work. We are so easily tempted to begin another task or to launch several projects simultaneously! We run faster and faster from one task to the other as we want to show and do the best we can, but the more projects we launch, the more we have to run, and the less time we have time to finish them on time, if at all!

We work hard in the hope of getting to rest after a completed task or project. We tell ourselves that things will be different when we have finished, but before we even finish, we let ourselves be tempted by an extra "small" assignment and another one and another one. However, you should know that the greatest joy takes place when finishing one assignment completely, instead of having a dozen assignments only half finished.

The experience of being able to concentrate fully and completely on one job is deeply more satisfying, and the result will therefore often be the best, both regarding the project and yourself.

While there is nothing wrong with being busy, and it is perfectly healthy to accept the challenges and development life can bring, it is pivotal to be aware of the way it affects you and your life. Perhaps you are not exactly thrilled about your job, but it is good knowing that you have something to wake up to in the morning. When you no longer feel that you have the power or an overview, then you must stop and figure out what it is that robs you of energy and makes you depressed, and from here you must question your work and leisure within yourself.

It is good to have a project or a job that we are passionate about. That in itself creates a spark, an enthusiasm, a development and not least an abundance of joy and other important aspects of our life - if you want!

It might also be possible that our job is not the only reason why we have too many projects going on at once, perhaps our precious leisure time is also to blame! When constantly planning new projects, we do not experience the liberty that we so much need to recharge and devote ourselves to nothing and yet still everything.

~ The family

Too many days or years dealing with everlasting and demanding tasks, may lead to a worn-out soul, one who do not have the energy or surplus to enjoy any other essential values in life; you collapse and let yourself be content with only dreaming of the green fields where the soul is allowed to run free and independently over the meadows, throwing itself joyously into the grass, rolling around and letting a laugh release the daily life.

Suddenly you wake up, and a tear is shed as the dream did not last long, even though it was truly where the soul wanted to be the most, its heart and desire.

Be aware that this does not have to remain only a dream, there is a possibility to make this a part of your life - but it is you, who must decide, and you who must take the first needed step. There is no limitation, only the one you put on yourself.

Many relationships or marriages dissolve due to lack of time and effort, each making us unable to keep the love alive. Each of us forget the beautiful and unique moments we have with our dear ones. The family, especially the children we brought into this world, must suffer under the pressure we let them grow up in. We want so badly to create the "perfect" physical frames and conditions, that we are unable to enjoy life together with the ones we love and care for, until these have been made. Unfortunately, the problem is that the time we spend creating these frames, we pay for expensively in hours and resources; the price is far too high, compared to precious moments we lose at the other end, and the supplementary bill is often impossible to pay. Often our children are the ones left behind to pay the bill, with the lack of their parents' closeness, complete presence and not least the absence of love and unique family moments. It is so wonderful being a couple or a family – imagine having the opportunity to share life with one another, some with the possibility of having children together and in that way becoming a family.

But being a couple, a family, or being single and having very close friendships, demands that everyone is cared for with attention and love. Nowadays, a relationship can very easily become affected by too much practical work, too many visits away from home and too many projects.

We each drift apart, and without knowing it in the first place, we let ourselves float further and further away from the common ground we met on, namely mutual love.

We take good care of the material things in our life, and the more we have, the more time it takes to maintain them, thus robbing us from important time we perhaps could have spent on each other.

In our race against time we forget to meet up along the way, to take our everyday life and existence together into account. Problems begins to afflict our families and relationships, and besides the struggle with the daily pressure, there is now another burden placed on top of the daily load that still needs to be lifted. Tired, we go to bed, side by side with our loved one, silent; with a mind influenced by sadness, darkness lowers into our hearts.

Thoughts wander in our inner soul, but lack of time and too many tasks means that we do not reach a solution to a potential controversy or disagreement, and the mountain of unsolved problems grows bigger and bigger – silently it tears two ever so close human hearts apart, laying in each side of their marriage bed, hiding away in their own thoughts. Volatile, they escape in dreams of how it could have been, and how they each would have liked it better in their mutual relationship.

Inevitably, two loving souls lose their feelings for one another, and slowly they become each other's burden instead of each other's strength.

Months or years can be lived this way, but the number of unsolved conflicts and the lack of mutual love and tenderness tears the skin to pieces on any one who let themselves be caught up in these patterns of life.

Finally, less and less is required, before one day, the tiniest thing at the "wrong" time may cause the bond to break, and two beautiful souls must separate with the loss of what, at the beginning, they had believed and hoped, namely to grow old together.

A bond between two people is strengthened by the love used to tie it with. The more weight and pressure placed on either end of this unique bond, the more loaded it becomes, and tiny little threads of hope and faith bursts. Slowly the bond becomes more and more fragile as we forget to repair and restore it with new, and maybe more solid threads, in order to strengthen it. Instead it bursts after a long time of too much pressure and lack of loving care and consideration.

Two souls are left with each half end of the bond, a bond once so beautifully knitted by hands in faith and love.

Many knitted bonds could have become stronger, and thereby remained tied if only we could become better at looking after them, with love and care. Together we must make them stronger, not weaken them.

~ The universal love

Whether being in a family, a couple, or being single, allow yourself to stop on your path of life, and ask yourself where you are going.

God granted you life with your inner soul and self that is pollinated with a complete, unique substance only known by your heart.
A strength is bestowed upon you, not just for you to show, but for you to use. We each have our strengths and weaknesses, and the more we live out love and listen to our inner selves, the longer and more richer a life we are then able to live.

This strength may appear in numerous ways and was given to you so that you would be able to take the steps needed in life, to reach the place where you belong. The place where you as a human being can live your life the best, with the gifts and love resident in you, and which are written in your heart.

Fear not when you go astray onto unknown paths, but explore them, study them, learn from them, even though they seem to come to a dead end. Your heart clearly sees the purpose God had to bring you to these places, considering your choices and decisions. Had God wanted us all to be alike, physically and mentally, he would have merely made copies of us.
But instead, in his love and wisdom, he made each individual soul different and completely unique, but with a common tone

of tune, that we all know and understand, which speaks every single dialect of the heart, namely the language of love. The language which we can't get around and ignore, no matter who and what we are.

Remember that the wings of love lift even the heaviest burdens in your mind; maybe you have just forgotten, maybe you have forgotten the road home…

The truth

*Indeed it is true that no one truth,
is more true than another
- as what may be the truth for you,
need not be the truth for others.*

We human beings may search many paths to find the truth in our lives.

Often, I am asked:
- What is the truth and what is not?

I usually give the answer:
- The truth that you feel is the right one.

How well do you know the desire to:

- Be well-intentioned, wanting to share with the whole world the truth you find right, and that brings you happiness?

- Want to tell and teach others how fantastic and wonderful your life has become since you found the truth and your path in life?

- Want to guide others down the same path which, for you, is filled with insight, love and wisdom?

- Want to share with others what has given you the strength to live a better life?

But instead you are met with silent resistance, anger or counter questions, as people do not agree with you, or maybe are just not ready to understand your insight!
Perhaps they feel that they have already found their truth, so are in no need of another.
Everything you experienced as the most beautiful and most truthful ever revealed, you are then made to feel was made into something others almost despised. They do not do so out of hatred or wickedness, but in self-defence – maybe they feel that it is more a matter of your needing to speak about it, than a matter of them wishing to hear it!

Dear you …
We are all different, and all at different stages in our lives.
We each find our own truth through our belief in the universe, nature, love or other sources that might bring us what we individually need in our search.

Everyone has need to make experiences in their own way.
Not least, the mind needs to discover on its own and be elevated in its blissful findings.

We must all give each other the freedom to decide and choose our own life's journey as all of us have different ways of searching for the insight into our lives.

We must each give room to everyone's lives, faith and choices in the respect of all of us being born in a common universe by

God, gifted with the free will of choosing on our own. Rather than condemning.

The art is not to be among those who have the same opinions as you; no, the art and power is to walk with wisdom and love, and to carry your truth in your heart amongst those who do not know, who do not believe, and maybe who not yet have found.

Do not engage in a discussion of what is the right or wrong truth. Keep silent in wisdom and listen in openness.

Show understanding and respect for other people's perhaps special choices of living.
Allow your inner self to understand that your truth is not up for discussion, but must be lived out and shared only with the ones who wish for it themselves.

Truth will not bear fruit by forcing your own belief onto your fellow human beings, but by granting them the freedom to decide for themselves.

Let your inner truth be expressed by actions of loves hands, not through the lips of noisy talk.

> *Just as many souls God has created,*
> *just as many truths there might be,*
> *also those we have not yet seen or found.*

The mind

I was once asked whether human beings can be born evil.
My reply to this was:
- God creates everything complete and with great care, therefore all he creates is made of love – including the children we bring into this world.

Although we are created in multiple colours and born in different places and environments, the aim for us is the same; that we learn to walk ourselves, so that we can individually wander through life, because no one can set our footprints.

However, children are influenced by their upbringing by their parents. It is the parents' task to guide their children in a positive direction and with love as the seat of honour.

It is essential that we, as parents, are an example of love – not only in words, but most importantly, in our actions.
Therefore it is important:

- That we try to cultivate our children's strengths, thereby giving them hope and belief in themselves, which is an important part of the plan and life.

- That we bring forth a desire to live, even in times of hardship.

- That we show them patience and remember that they are

young, and only just have started their learning.

- That we give them the freedom to feel on their own what is right and wrong, based on what they are here and now.

One of the reasons many people do not know how to listen to their hearts, is that they have completely forgotten to listen to what was given to them from the beginning – namely a mouthpiece, leading them on their way forward.

There is no use in trying to shape our children based on our own needs, instead we need to try to listen to their needs. They are not others, and they are not us, they are what God made them to be from the beginning – small, sensitive seeds, who shall develop with a heart of purity.
Teach them a guide to life with love and without punishment
Support them and show them the way, by being a good example yourself.

It may be difficult as a parent to know when we help and guide our children the best – without crossing their emotional boundaries. But a good starting point is to figure out when we need to fulfil our owns need to help our children, as opposed to when it is the child's need of help - what may feel so right to you, may perhaps not feel right for your child.

Love them for their own unique personality, and give them the strength to feel that they have the strength and courage to pursue life's many levels of choices.

It is important not to think of ourselves as bad parents when our children choose something different from what we thought was right for them, and remember what a gift they are given, when they themselves get the opportunity to test boundaries with their own mind.

We have to remember the way we ourselves have grown, the steps we took that led us to what we have become today - namely the steps that led us to our own experiences.

The child who is being carried on the arm for too long in life, will not learn to walk itself.

As parents, we have to be careful not to hold their wings so tight and hard that they will never fully grow and become whole and strong - in that way their wings would not be able to carry them through life, to fly freely.

God does not create birds without a complete set of wings – how would they be able to survive in this world?

Children are the beginning of a new life.
They are wonderfully curious and have an innate desire to examine all of life's subtleties in length and breadth. They are driven by the zest for life and have no anxiety or prejudice to begin with; they are totally open, pure and vulnerable.

They have no words, their only communication out in this world is through crying or laughing.

They have an innate purity, so let this purity be reciprocated with love and wisdom.
Whether they are children or teenagers, they are still on their way to becoming beautiful flowers, only they do not yet know which flower they are, or when they have fully blossomed.
Give them the freedom they may need, and love them for their wonderful way of being as they are seeds too, sown by the hands of God.

Daring to set foot on new paths

It may feel so difficult, daring to tread the new paths that life grants. To have the courage to let go of what seems to be the safe path.

> *Better stay on the path of pain and agony*
> *than daring to walk along new, unknown, free*
> *and happy paths.*

Dear you …
Have you forgotten that life was given to you, for you to live it?
Do not compromise your precious soul and heart.
When you feel that you are locked up and chained by hand and foot, and feel that you no longer can live your day fully and completely, you must remember to take care of your inner flower. Otherwise it will slowly wither and no longer be able to grow or blossom, or able to spread new seeds.
Do you understand? A flower can grow in the most muddy, windswept and barren places, but it desperately craves light and water.
If you no longer have the strength to create the needed energy to form this most important nourishment to your inner flower, then time has come to find another way or solution, in order for you to give it the best growing conditions.
The flower that before seemed lost, will get stronger and more beautiful, and then with exaltation it will rise in bloom and let its petals unfold.

And you, dear you …!
You will once again find your happiness by being able to enjoy the essentials in life. Namely the sight and fragrance of your inner flower's strength, and you will feel a sincere inner satisfaction and balance when you see your flower of life in blossom!

Keep in mind that nobody has the power to limit you, unless you yourself give them the power to do so.
You are accountable for your life and your heart, as it is you, and only you, who are the bearer of it.
Do not allow those around you to rob you of this elixir of life which was especially made for you, and just awaits you having the courage to drink of it.

*Do not think of what might limit you,
but how you can liberate yourself.*

How far will you let yourself carry this burden that overloads and inhibits your steps in life? How much are you ready to sacrifice, and give away your own life-energy?

*What is the use of travelling the world to seek freedom
if you are a prison inside.
When there are people sitting in prison,
who are able to feel freedom.*

Maybe you have forgotten the fragrance of life's oxygen and

aromas, floating freely around you wherever you go. All you need to do is breathe calmly, and you will receive the most wonderful sensation of life's gifts of fragrances.

Have you forgotten the feeling of stopping and setting up camp on your wander and search in life, so that the next day you can get up and feel that every day you tread a fantastic and living organism called Earth, and notice that it contains and surrounds us with all the elements that God has created, so that you and I can exist in all nuances of life.
It is given to you freely and without charge, only with the sincere wish that you discover it and let yourself be nourished by it. And hereby you can live and rejoice in harmony with your life in this world.

The very moment you were placed in this world, you were given free will, but at the same time you were also handed a responsibility for your life in the future.

Nobody can deprive you your soul, unless you let them.

Your soul is not for sale - no price is high enough, as the nourishment you can give it has been given to you without conditions and free of charge.

Find your path in life

Having a direction in life is the best for you as a human being, in order for you to live a harmonious, loving and meaningful life, so that:

- You can obtain the complete feeling of liberty, without being restrained by what others mean or think about you.

- You can live in accordance with your heart, thereby acting out what feels right for you, without being limited by yourself or others.

- You are able to live in the present, to feel love for everything and thereby obtain fulfilment.

It may be a long journey finding one's life's direction, and following it whole-heartedly. At times it may feel lonely, as only you and your soul can walk the often winding paths leading to your goal.
Now and then the consequence may be that you have to leave people and material things behind.
This can be a painful decision, as you may feel that you are hurting your fellow beings.
However, you are not acting out of wickedness, but merely because you are seeking new paths and a greater understanding of yourself and your life.

Imagine that your life journey is the road ahead of you, long and unknown. On that road you will pass many incidents and people. Sometimes people stay on your road for a long time, at other times they pass in just a few seconds or minutes.

We are influenced by these many encounters, whether they are beautiful or traumatic. While walking, we pick up impressions and experiences for our life's journey so that we carry in our backpack all that might affect us in our mind and heart.

The art is not just of collecting stuff, but also clearing out your backpack and letting go of what there no longer seems room for, otherwise the burden becomes too heavy to bear, and might occupy space for new and exciting things, waiting to be discovered and caught in your hands.

However, it is important to keep the essential and significant things. By that I mean that you must not, or do not need to, let yourself be weighed down by the worst memories of your past, nor must you let yourself be defeated by them. Instead, learn from the past, so that you are able to bring it with you as a strength and experience in the future.

So when you feel your backpack becomes too heavy, and you are so burdened by it that you can not walk, or in some cases not even move, then you have to go through the contents and sort it out.

Let go of what you no longer need to carry, give it its freedom and let it wander out of your hands, in the belief that the universe of God will let something else be shown to you. Something new and maybe more useful for you that will strengthen you on your journey ahead.

The fewer heavy burdens occupying space in your life's backpack, the more space there will be for love and its many parcels.

It may be difficult to stay on life's path as it is tempting to let oneself be carried away into the direction of others' lives. But the intention is not for you to wander their journeys, thereby living their lives. If you live your life with one leg in each, then it will be half a you, half a heart and therefore a half-lived life.

So when you have lost your direction in life, and it does not feel right to you anymore, and when you feel that, although you are walking and walking, the steps are not yours, then you have come too far away from home - too far away from your course of life.

To offer help and let go afterwards

Many times I have been asked, how I am able to have so many people coming into my life - people with unfortunate destinies and sad historic backgrounds of various types, without me myself becoming wearied or sad.

When an unhappy soul has come to me for comfort and guidance to get on with life, I walk on the sidelines with them. Listening, reading and feeling for them throughout the course, while they are with me.
I walk through their pain and suffering, together with them. You may say that I travel with them in their lives as a spectator and participant on the sideline. I relate to them as human beings and the destinies they have, and from that I am able to give advice and guidance.
Showing them the way, when they have come too far away from home.

But it is most important that when I have finished listening, watching and guiding, that they themselves must walk from here.
I let them go in the belief that I have done what I can to the best of my ability, and so I place this human being's soul in the hands of God. Knowing that He will embrace this person and always stay by their side, unconditionally.

It is most essential to remember that if you would like to be helpful to a soul, it is of no use to let yourself be weighed down by their problems and let yourself get carried away. If someone's life is in confusion and unhappiness, it is no good if you also let yourself get confused and unhappy and bring yourself down..

For who is then to help lift the weak one?

The trials of life

*God does not want to make your life tougher,
but to strengthen you,
to the tough times in life.*

Often the worst headwinds and hurricanes in our life feels like our lowest point.

I have been asked whether this is God punishing us?
I smile lovingly, and reply:

- God does not punish us, he just shows us the consequences of the decisions and actions we make in our life.

The trials we are introduced to are trials of strength, or some kind of task for us to handle or solve. Precisely for us to be strengthened for the future tasks in life.
If we do not pass them the first time around, we are certain to be introduced to them again, until we have learned to handle them correctly, acting from the heart and soul we carry inside of us.

I consider ourselves rather as gardeners, each having our piece of garden to cultivate.
By that I mean that God from the beginning has granted us a piece of earth as a foundation which we can cultivate according to our own choice and ability.

The healthier soil we cultivate, the healthier fruit we harvest. God has given you the seeds and best growing conditions for you to cultivate the land.

When we make up our minds to become better gardeners, that is to say, better human beings, we have to examine which kind of soil we have been given.
It is no use examining what others or our the neighbours have been given as this is not your soil!

Having to accept that there are too many weeds in your soil can be tough - but if you want to plant something new and make it grow, you have to begin by turning the soil around and cultivating it, in order to remove the weed completely.
It may be tough demanding work. It is messy and demands a lot of energy as you have to dig up the roots of life's problems, otherwise they will strangle the new ones that are sown. The sooner you get rid of the weed the better, as it has not yet had time to grow roots and therefore comes out much easier.

This is also the case with life's problems; the sooner we try to solve them, the easier they let go. Otherwise they may begin to grow and spread, thereby causing more and bigger problems. While working in your garden, toiling and labouring, you must know that God is always with you. He does not deceive you, he feels for you and is constantly by your side, even when you feel the most forsaken and exhausted.

He is the master gardener and will willingly teach you the art of making ready for life in your garden.
But you are the one to perform the job!

This process is meant for you. You are the one to feel the pain of how lonely it may be when nothing visible has yet grown in your garden. This may result in a reluctance to go on. And it might be very tempting to begin to re-grow the old crops, still standing here and there, neither big, nor nourishing for life, but seemingly safe because you know them.

The choice of daring to let go takes time and demands courage in order to learn a new, better and more beautiful way of cultivating life's flowers and fruits, which in addition will give you fruit and nourishment all your life, if you remember to take care of them!

Life's processes can be compared with a compost heap. All the weed we collect in our gardens, and all that seems to be dangerous for our beautiful roses, are our life's traumas and pain. All these weeds we then gather and put into our compost - thereby allowing a process to begin.

While processing, it may at times seem as the heap will dissolve completely. The fear of everything disappearing and nothing being left often make our minds worry, and everything may feel terrible, so completely and utterly hopeless.

It is to no use if halfway through the process we remove the content, trying to save it or put it to use, because the process is only halfway through and merely in decay.

But if we arm ourselves with patience and let the process go its full course, then the result will be the finest, most vigorous and fertile soil, so with care, relief and joy, we can share it with our own and others' roses.

༄

Decisions

It feels wonderfully liberating to finally make a decision that has been on its way for a long time, in the form of many thoughts, being weighed back and forth on many nights..
Thoughts in favour of and thoughts against your decision. But very often you will in realize with hindsight that it was your very first impulse that was right for you.

Dear you ...
If you are at a point in your life where you feel it is time for a change, then it is also time to make a decision on how to change – because it is by making decisions that you change and embark on new paths, with new opportunities presenting themselves.

Regardless of which situation you might find yourself in, it is only a decision from the heart that can take you further from where you currently stand.

You may seek help and guidance from your loved ones or others, but as only you are the one responsible for your life, only you can arrive at a decision, the one that is right for you.

Although you are not fully aware of the consequences of a major decision, it is important for you and your life that you make a decision, not just in words, but more importantly, by your actions and standing by it. Despite those around you perhaps speaking against it, and not seeing it as the right decision you have made, allow yourself to walk the path you have decided – if it feels right in your heart, then it is the right path for you.

Understand the truth, in that every time you make a decision or make a choice in your life, it will always have a consequence, therefore it is important that you feel and ask yourself whether you are ready to accept this consequence. Not because it will necessarily be bad, but because it may turn out differently than you had expected – however, it will always be right, based on the choice you have made.

Do not make your decisions under too much pressure or with too much noise around you, as this will only disturb your clarity of thought and judgement.

Decisions may drain you of energy, but they are essential for you as they create openings and new challenges in your life. And most importantly, they take part in shaping your life.

The smallest decisions,
may make the biggest differences.

Patience

An apple sat so beautifully on a twig of branch.
Hanging with the weight of its juices, by its stem,
not yet ripe, but round and full in its natural form.
Surrounded and sheltered,
the apple was embraced by leaves so green.
Let itself be warmed
and delighted by the glow of sunbeams.
Lived in its all and now, grew
and let its shell become strong,
in harmony with its Lord, the tree.
For days, rain and wind ruled,
overshadowing the sun's caresses of the apple.
Finally the sky opened,
and the earth invited the Sun with all its glory.
The crisp apple courted when the Sun again made its entrance,
and let itself blush in the warm company.
The Summer waned,
and the apple itself seemed to be at its height,
in size and strength.
Hanging there, impatiently,

rocking in time with the light breeze,

it felt ripe for departure.

But very well it knew in its deepest seed of heart

that Mother Tree did not let go its fruit until it was time!

The apple asked carefully the vigorous tree:

Why can I not just go now?

The tree swaying in its thoughts for an answer:

Because, my dear child!

If I let you go now, you will be bitter in taste,

dry in your flesh and without vitamins in your strength,

and therefore not ripe for your journey to the hungry mouths.

I spare you meeting the world,

so it will not become a fall as your worst moment.

I will rather give you all the time you might need to become ripe,

so in the hour of your departure,

you will be sent away with love,

strengthened and ripe,

not until then will you be able to bring strength

and a juice of divine taste from the universal basket of fruit.

Placed in a trunk, born on a twig of branch,

and ripened fully and completely in the spirit of God's time.

Patience is an important source to a harmonious and peaceful life – as time heals many wounds by itself and works on what you are waiting for in the moments you might be resting.

Patience pays off, in time maturing, and developing what we have had to wait for.
Time is in constant motion, and a lot is underway in every second as an answer, or as a creation of what has been set to grow.

Far too many detours are often made in our attempt to reach our destination faster.
Unfortunately, in our eagerness we may instead force things through and thereby ruin them for ourselves; we may become desperate and scared that it may disappear out of our hands if we do not do something. Unhappy and regretful, we are left annoyed with having to settle for half, as well as realising that had we but waited, all would have fallen into place, probably all by itself.

If we become ill, we have a tendency to let ourselves be stressed by the thoughts of what we can not get done, and what we should be doing, while lying in our sickbed.
The result only being that without considering it, we add further strain on body and soul, thereby prolonging the process of healing – as we steal the time and energy that our immune system needs so much to recover.
And should we rise before time has healed our body, the illness

may come back twofold and just demand an even longer time in the sickbed.

We may become afraid of life passing us by, if we do not step in and act immediately. Persistently, we try to influence the course of events, wanting to steer and thereby obtaining the control that in no way do we have the ability to master.

Often we burden ourselves with unnecessary, destructive thoughts as we seem to thrive best when we have the answer to the questions that might occupy our mind.
Do not let your time be spent on producing scary scenarios of what you do not yet know.

Do not let yourself be broken down by sleepless nights while you wait for an answer.
Instead, accept that what shall come, will come – and that it will come, when it is time, if it is time.
And if it does not come, it was not meant to be.

Dear you …
Wait patiently until the answer itself makes its entrance, and only then can you consider and relate to your situation.
It is much easier to wait until you have something concrete to take a position on – as you can not relate to something that is not there.

Each of us has our own pace, and you have yours.

Do not attempt to hurry yourself when others grow impatient. It is important for you to take the necessary time, in order for you to accomplish your goal.
Likewise, you have to give those around you the time they might need, whether they are children or adults.

Patience completes what has been sown and planted – if in your eagerness you try to hasten its growth with too much fertilizer, you might risk stifling what was set out to grow, thereby never seeing which flower would have flourished. If only it had been planted by a hand of patience …

It is understandable that it is difficult to keep calm while waiting, but often it is by far the best, as the waves have to calm down before you can sail further on again.
In your impatience, you might risk setting out into a storm and a battle that might in the end result in you capsizing, and then having to swim all the way back anyway, perhaps even returning at last to the exact same starting point, but empty-handed!

Patience provides room for those around you to take the time they need. It does not push angrily, or disturb the one who needs peace in their time of reflection.

It waits until a moment of anger has passed so that with peace and love in mind, it may consider what subsequently might need to be said, if anything should be said.

Thus it only speaks after having collected itself.

Patience does not push the ones standing in front. It always waits its turn.

Patience does not choose easy short cuts. It walks the roads necessary, no matter how difficult and painful they might be, in order to reach its goal with pride.

Patience always completes the task it has taken on, in the best possible way. Should the task prove to be too big or overwhelming, it must ask for help.

It does not attempt to hurry the passage of life, by forcing the process needed. With patience it collects even the smallest seeds, in order to finally be able to create a life in full harmonious growth.

> *Patience is the pulse, beating the important beats of your life's heart.*

Dear divinity

Dear divinty...

Raise in me my holy temple,
rebuild what may have fallen
and let nothing get lost therein

Light every candle,
that only is alive with its last ember,
and let its glow once again
illuminate every dark place

Raise in me felicity
and let it eliminate any destructive and negative
thought
that may have taken residence in me

Let my mind run after hope,
rather than sinking deep into despair

Give me strength in the most difficult moments of
forgiveness,
and release those spirits
I might have tied, with my ego-limiting ties

Raise in me, faith and strength.
Be with me,
in all my many steps, on my many roads,
towards you

*Forgive me if I stumble, and do not become
tired of having to reach me,
your precious patience,
that raises me in life
and enables me to continue walking*

*Allow my eyes to see through yours,
and show me the way when everything seems
blurred of a heavy, heavy fog of despair*

*Forgive me for the times I may end up on
misleading paths
and temptation's dead end*

*I beg you humbly,
be persistent in your calling, when my ears
seem deaf
to your voice, shout!
With a voice of thunder,
if you may need to*

*I beg you through my remorse and in my
deepest humility,
of life and in spirit,
do not abandon me, despite my many mistakes
do not cease to call on me,
so I can find the way home to you*

*Thank you for tirelessly
holding my light,
when I, due to my weaknesses,
are not capable of holding it myself*

*Thank you for bearing with me,
for all the times I forgot to give you thanks,
or did not understand to praise the blessings,
you unceasingly,
bestow upon mine and others lives*

*Oh divine!
Thank you for embracing anyone,
who might need your endless all-embracing
love,
regardless of colour, life or faith*

*I bend for you, my face,
in my devotion and gratitude,
for everything you in spirit bestow
and in life, makes possible for me*

*I seek my sanctuary at your feet,
and seek my shelter, through my deeds and
thoughts through you,
for the joy and benefit
of other living creatures,
than me...*

Dear divinity

Be true to your feelings

Feelings are in constant movement – like the ocean that sometimes foams and rises high in a gale, that lets itself fall and once again becomes one with the salty water. Other times so quiet and beautiful that everything seems to be reflected in it. So calm, smooth and almost completely untouched, without a single scratch on its surface.
But at the slightest touch – this vulnerable surface will at once react with a movement – in the form of rings, wavering to the shores of love in all directions.
An undercurrent in the depths of the ocean has begun its journey, a journey into the feelings of time.

A human being is made of flesh, blood and spirit. Plus an undefinable thing which is its own, and which all the way through is moved by what it is in or surrounded by. The word being: feelings.

How well do you know the feeling of pain, the times where you have had to renounce something, or someone you maybe loved – the feeling of being nailed to the floor by thoughts that deprived you of your spark of life, and the joy of living?

Which constantly trigger you to run down the corridors of fearfulness, always being on your way, only to avoid meeting the face of your heart and feelings with the eyes of truth that you do not yet have the courage to look into.

Frightened, you turn away your eyes, to avoid what speaks to your heart, and which with a confrontation would call you to account for your past actions.

Dear you ...
Fear not, and do not despair!
Feelings are the road forward to reconciliation with the depths of your heart, and a higher understanding of yourself.

Feelings exists in all aspects, in all forms, strengths and lengths, but only with one target: love. You must take your feeling by the hand, so that on a mutual walk together you will learn to understand each other. So that together you may learn to speak the same language, thus the book of your heart will be written in your mind, and later become the reference book you may seek help from.

It is very important that you are true to your feelings, and that you walk with them all the way. Then they need not haunt you suddenly and unannounced, and often emerge inconveniently, thereby causing you anxiety or anger.

It is important that you allow yourself to stay with your feelings as long as necessary, as it is only by your acceptance and understanding that you will be able to fully act this out.

There are times you might feel it repeating, in the form of a recurring feeling, then make sure to welcome it without fear and irritation. Once more you will have to walk alongside it, asking it additional questions.
Cry or be angry if necessary, but persistently you must keep in contact with your feelings. For they always bring you a message that is important, for you to walk with more strength in the future. And you will become wiser from the discoveries of your mind. You must never fail the feeling of your heart, in spite of other people's lack of understanding in their desire to impose on you the same feelings that they have. The feeling is yours, and nobody feels it better than you do.

In your most vulnerable and tired moments you must not try to change your feelings, in order to get others to like you better. Since when you are alone, feelings will call you to account in consultation with you and your heart.

Let yourself understand that they are not your enemy, but a friend of your heart, soul and life.
The times they bring you to your knees is to get you to see and thereby gain insight into your inner universe of love's understanding.

Trust your feelings, especially in the moments where it seems frightening that it may seem strange to your mind, but is so well-known by your heart ...

You may try to repress them, but you can not get around it. They haves found an eternal home in you, coloured by your choices and experiences of your life.
Otherwise you may get the impression that they are almost fighting your life and soul. As if they want you to reach the understanding of their existence and messages with the voice of your inner self.
Happily you will come to the understanding that they will be by your side forever, and will never deceive you. Their strength being of a kind that can not be expressed in the form of numbers, or be issued as a written proof, a certificate to others. Only to you, as you are the owner, and also the recipient, of the presents you make yourself worthy of.

Let yourself come to the understanding that you are dependent on your feelings, in order to find your own way to freedom.
You may find your own unique way of living, find your own personal style, in togetherness with yourself, others and the life you might yourself form, as long as you yourself can vouch for it, and feel an inner happiness and satisfaction by it.
Your feelings want you to understand that you cannot repress them, regardless of whether you are working, travelling or in other ways trying to escape them. So therefore, let yourself remember that they are not there to hinder you in life, but on the contrary, to teach you to how to live it.

So do not fight them, but wear them with pride and pleasure, stay confident about them, no matter how much they might hurt, and which roads they might lead you on. Because the roads you have walked and must walk in the future, are the roads that leads you to who you potentially are.

Live according to the book of your heart, in which every experience has left its marks in the sign of a feeling. These signs will become a text that only you can read – but with strong glasses that carry your heart's message.

> *For it is not a matter of you having to change*
> *your feelings, but about the way,*
> *you live them out and act with them*
> *- in relation to yourself and your surroundings.*

Self-knowledge

*It is a great strength to acknowledge one's
vulnerabilities and weaknesses,
but a big weakness,
having the need to show one's strength.
As we have been given the strength to use it,
not to show it ...*

It is never a good feeling having to acknowledge our own mistakes.
We do not like having to look at the side of ourselves, the side we dislike.
It may feel humiliating if others see what we prefer not to see in ourselves.
Often we would rather not be confronted with our dark side as it makes us feel like a weak person, having to face the truth of being vulnerable – we seem to thrive best being strong outwardly.

But it is ever so important that we take hold of ourselves when imbalances occur that lead us into situations which make us angry or unhappy.
We are sensitive individuals, who sense and react to our surroundings.
We try our best to act correctly, but certain situations may get us into fierce and hateful states of mind, causing us to offend

or hurt the ones involved.

When situations arise that makes us angry or unhappy, it immediately seems easier to place the responsibility for our own actions on others.

But dear you …

Others can not become the cause of your or my anger or the unhappiness we might bear in our heart, unless we permit it!

You will have to go back in time, although it will probably feel unpleasant. You must to try to figure out what brought you into this state of mind.

To the best of your ability, try to be honest to yourself, and acknowledge the wrongs you did yourself, knowing well that you did not do it on purpose, and that at the time you were not aware of the consequences it could have on you and those around you. But something went wrong, and the only way to release this pain in you is by obtaining self-knowledge.

Often we have to suffer pain before understanding what it is that we are no good at handling in relation to other people. One of the most frequent and difficult causes is that we forget to listen to our inner feelings, thereby completely forgetting to set our own boundaries. But it is so immensely important that we are able to draw these lines.

If we do not draw them, they will time and time again be crossed which may lead us to react fiercely in anger and frustration towards the ones crossing them, and in the end, it is ourselves we get angry with as we allowed our boundaries to be exceeded once again. Those around us are seldom able to see our invisible boundaries, if we do not show them to them...

> *How are those around you to relate to your boundaries, if you yourself are not able to?*
> *How are they to relate to you,*
> *if you do not relate to yourself?*

It is of no use expecting the people around us to change before we ourselves can get better. Each of us has to acknowledge that if anything has to be changed, we have to begin with ourselves as the right starting point.

It is an elevating feeling being allowed to help others that might need help. It helps us to feel valuable and useful.
We must only remember to draw attention to where the line must be drawn, and how much and for how long time we can assist.
Otherwise sad and hurtful episodes may occur, spoiling even the strongest friendship.
The person offering a helping hand may suddenly feel exploited and misused, and an uneasy atmosphere spreads both on the inside and out – causing disharmony to arise.
It is such a pity and often also undermining when we forget to respect our own inner boundaries, or when we do not respect those of others. A lot of misunderstandings could be avoided, if we just understood and realized the importance of speaking

clearly before everything gets blurry and vague.

Yes, you can change yourself! But trying to cheat your inner soul? No! You can not change what you are, deep down in your soul ...

Accept who you are, and learn that others can not become responsible for the decisions you make, even if you let them talk you into something.

You can release yourself from the burden of expectations, by merely acknowledging that in fact you might have too big expectations of those around you, and perhaps also of yourself. Feel the freedom you bring into your life by walking to the door of self-knowledge, and there receiving the tasks that may help in releasing you from many bitter and unhappy moments.

Self-knowledge is the medicine that can clear your soul and mind from anger, as well as free you from the feeling of being a victim of other people's lack of understanding and insight into your inner personality.

> *How are others to come to an understanding of you, if you do not understand yourself?*

In order to realize the truth about yourself, you will have to search deep inside your conscience, in harmony with your heart.

Only then you will find the answer as to how you are best able to act with love and politely in the future without causing disharmony to those around you.

If we constantly allow our lives to be overshadowed by the feeling that those around us are to blame for our dark moments, the sunbeams will never reach their way to our hearts and minds – as we perhaps ourselves are in the shadow of the sun.

> *What is the use of our Lord letting the sun shine upon our path, if we choose the shadow?*

What you send out

*Millions of thoughts are travelling this very
moment. On their way out,
sent and posted by human minds.
Millions of decisions and actions travel
criss-crossing through time and space.
Set into motion, and on the basis of man's
own thought and action of hands.
All on its way out, with messages, and questions
of any kind,
only to later return with an answer to the sender ...*

It is very enriching, and we may become extremely happy when we receive presents from life's gift box. Presents that brings happiness and light into our lives and mind. The experience of loving fellow beings who reach out a hand when we need it the most, can inspire hope, and a desire that we ourselves want to contribute to life. It might also be people coming to thank you, in gratitude for your help long ago.
Innumerable moments could be mentioned which bring joy into our hearts.

It is a great pleasure and joy when we are rewarded for the deeds we perform in life, be it a salary for the work we do in our daily life, or thanks for what we have given with a helping hand.

The optimism seems to be greatest when we are aware in advance that some sort of salary awaits for the task we have willingly taken on.
And the disappointment is huge if we feel that our work is not properly appreciated.

But life gives in accordance with the profit we ourselves have contributed, nor is it certain that we will always receive a thank you or thank-you gifts, but surely, some day we will be rewarded, but perhaps in a way we did not expect.

When we make an effort and give from ourselves, we have to do it sincerely and without expectation, because then we do not feel disappointment, but are rewarded in the life of our own heart.

The universe remembers the moments where a soul gives from an unconditional and pure heart. The name of that human will be remembered, till the day he or she might themselves be in need of a helping hand.
The more pure and wholeheartedly you offer yourself with your own hand, the more you can make yourself worthy of deserving.

It is not always certain that what you offer comes back immediately with thanks.
But it is certain that it is remembered in the heart of the universe, and that you shall receive it in the very moment you

yourself might need it, and maybe least expect it …

We all get what we deserve, for the virtues we perform, but if you are helping others solely in order to manipulate or control, or in order to get attention for your deed, then it is not given unconditionally, but with the aim of reaping the benefits for yourself!

Do not think of what you might obtain, with what you send off, but of the spirit and intention that you send it with – what you send off will, at some point, return as answers to your virtues. Be it in words, thoughts or actions.

Give! And you shall be given, when you may need.

Receive! And other will receive you.

Love! And you may be loved for your love.

The art is not to embrace and give to the ones who love you.
The art consists of giving love from a pure heart,
to the ones who do not understand and do not love you.

Anger

Anger and love appear to be opposites, both with their own target and message.

As love creates, redeems and provides opportunities, so anger limits, destroys and hampers love.

And yet in spite of their differences, they seem to have a common denominator, namely that they both make a big difference in this world!

Anger can leave the deepest tracks behind it. It rules and reacts and likes to fight big battles in order to obtain power and control. It may be so impotent that it kills everything that may be around it, because its hidden source – powerlessness – pushes the anger forwards and uses it as its shield, to keep those around it at distance. With a sudden stroke, it is able to transform even the sunniest day into the darkest night.

Anger is the most unpleasant and destructive feeling we can have in us as it destroys any peace and disturbs any harmonious atmosphere there might be.

It is destructive because it poisons our existence, and denies access to any reasonable thought, depriving its owner of his or her judgement.

Anger and inner hate may provoke the most serious illnesses and may therefore shorten our precious lives, if given the power!

It may be the cause of people who live together having to separate and part company, as anger is terrifying and subversive to the love that is essential in a relationship.

Its character may be so violent that other people choose to keep at a distance, thus avoiding any kind of contact with the one who is ruled by his/her anger. It gets lonely – as other around them choose to do without them because of a lack of confidence and maybe even fear of their violent actions.

If anger is allowed to dominate our lives, there is a big risk that it will develop into something monstrous or catastrophic. This tendency will intensify, if we do not confront it and fight its existence.

Dear you ...
If your life and mind are poisoned by anger, hatred and intolerance , then you must try to figure out when and in which situations these feelings arises. You must realize that this anger ruins your life, and eradicates any peace for you, as it undermines your relations with your fellow human beings. You must try to eliminate your anger – you must root it out, as it is a weed trying to suffocate the flowers surrounding you so beautifully.

Feel the sadness and limitations it creates in you, not least the chaos it brings into your life.

It is your life, and you are the one to master it; do not let yourself accept your anger or your hate as the things that rule and dominate your life.

With all your strength and reflection, you must examine where the root of your anger stems from, you must go back into your past and call it into account – because if you do not pull it out at the root, it will still be able to spread in your mind, and still be able to continue to rule your life.

It may be incidents from your upbringing that have planted the first seed of an internal hate. It may be situations where you have felt humiliated because you were not respected, or maybe you were brought up in an environment where anger ruled your daily life.
It may also be traumatic events, having provoked a sort of contempt and lack of respect and confidence to those around you. Several causes from your past may play an important role in the present, and trigger your anger; however, it is important that you try to figure out where in life the first seed of hate was sown, with all of your might, and all of your perseverance.

When, through self-discovery, you have established the reason for your anger, you must firmly decide in your mind that whatever situation you face in the future, you will no longer react with anger – but instead stay calm and controlled with a strength of tolerance, patience and peace of mind.

Then love and joy may once again emerge on your path ahead, and you may now wander freely. A new era can begin for you, and you can start over on a happy life - because anger did not get the power and reign over your life.

> *Plant a flower in your inner soul, every time you conquer*
> *your anger, create a sea of flowers.*
> *Share with the ones, you wish love,*
> *give in abundance*
> *— for every time a flower is given, you give pleasure*
> *to the heart of a soul.*

Anxiety

Anxiety may be very limiting in life.
It is like a parasite crawling around in your body, sponging off and ruling your inner thoughts. It seems to be able to eradicate any form of growth of inner joy.
It is nourished by past memories which inflicted sufferings, and traumatic experiences, either of an emotional or physical character.
The more it is fed with doubt and restricting thoughts, the bigger it grows. It hampers any healthy growth of peace, and sucks out any energy needed for the daily activities of life.
It may be active at all hours of the day, and the more time and attention it is given, the less sleep it permits.
It wants to force you to your knees, making you submit to its dominance – so that you do not dare to live your life as you sincerely wish it. Anxiety prefers you to choose a life behind bars in its company, thereby permitting it to deprive you from life and any chance of growth of self-worth.

Dear you …
Do not let your inner anxiety reject the peace that you so deeply wish in your life. Grasp the beauty and let it light up your inner room of anxiety which through time has been haunted by the dark thoughts of your mind.

When you feel that anxiety tries to dominate your life, and you are about to lose any form of rationality, it is time for you to confront it and look directly into its eyes – grasp the sword of courage and cut off its invisible tentacles which for so long, and persistently have been holding you back.

Let it no longer lead you towards doubt when the truth of love appears. Banish it, and do not give into previously known thoughts of pain; let your inner light of hope restore the belief in your self-worth – as doubt and darkness are the basic sources of the survival of anxiety.

At times, anxiety may even be so strong that it can lead your life all the way to the abyss. As it blinds your faith in a better life, a life just waiting for you to dare to take the full step, resolutely walk toward it with faith in your heart.

Do not let yourself continue to be a slave of your fear which whips and punishes you every time you dare to take just one step towards hope, as its only aim is to make you unable to get up and leave it.

Do not let yourself be misled by fear's conviction that your life can not be lived without it by your side – the truth being that it is fear and anxiety which are dependent on you and your attention, otherwise they will die!

Anxiety may be the fear of what you do not know and can not see.

Anxiety, may be the fear of fear.

❧

Suffering and Pain

A soul stands on its life's middle.
Beholding the world, letting the thoughts wander
back to the moments of life, having
left their mark.
Immediately invisible on the outside – but quite perceptible
and visible on the inside, the sufferings and pains of the past
have forever taken residence in a firmly cemented memory
to be used as learning, later on.
Sensing the wind on its face, feeling the earth
underneath its feet.
A life is on its way, having stopped – taking stock of
what has been, what is now, and prepared
for what might come.
For what has been were seeds being collected.
What is here and now, is where they shall grow.
And what will come, is what will grow
from the seeds, sown by the pains and trials
of the past.

It can be so difficult to understand why certain people at times have to be exposed to so much pain, and have to climb so many heights in the mountains of suffering.

Some fight enormous battles and often have emotional difficulties. It seems as if they are wandering in shoes of lead, and therefore burdened with heavy and very difficult steps throughout their lives.

While others lives may seem easier and less painless, as if they have wings, and can soar easily through their lives.

However, we are all marked and influenced by the experiences life has given us.

Our differences and our individual choice of lifestyle results in us being assigned different tasks in life, not least of different character. We may choose to look at our visit on earth as a kind of schooling where we may learn lessons based on who we are and what we come from.

So every decision we make is followed by a task that only we can solve, with help and possible guidance along the way if we need it.

In case we are unable to fully completely the task the first time around, then we have to, once more, and perhaps with even greater difficulties, repeat the task, only in another way.

It may feel unmercifully, tiresome and not least frustrating having to toil through the same themes once more. Especially when we were convinced that we had learned – and therefore were sure to have passed the 'test'.

Instead we must realize in our hearts that we did not learn from the pain we previously went through, and that we have to go through it once more.

It may hurt in our soul but it is important, and at times vital, in order to learn and be strengthened for our life and other tasks ahead.

The lowest downturn can become the highest ascent in your life.

I have often been asked:
- Why is the difference so huge between us?

- Why do certain people have to suffer so much?

- Why does God not treat us equally?

My answer to this is:
- That the pain that might rule in this world is not of God's wish but, unfortunately, created by the decisions we human beings have made and will make in the future.

His wish is not for us to suffer, but to learn, so that we are able to wander strengthened through our lives and pass the assignments handed to us.

We have been granted free will as a present, enabling us to choose freely. Often we are faced with choices leading us in two different directions, both unknown!

Unfortunately, we are not always able to choose what is the best for us or our fellow beings, but we choose what we think is the best.

In politics or other correlations, decisions are made that are not always the most favourable for all human beings, where the consequences may lead to war, starvation and illnesses, thereby causing suffering and pain.

The same applies when we ourselves make decisions, that we sometimes choose the 'easy' way out, perhaps because we are in a moment of time constraint and therefore choose the "easy" and "fastest" way, right now.

However, the result may end up tedious and being a far more troublesome and painful way, than had we chosen the other solution, which originally seemed more demanding, but which in the end proved to be the easiest, most valid and in reality, maybe the best way.

> *Often the fastest and easiest solutions might be the ones, that are the least valid and might take the longest time.*

Unfortunately, we are not always able to listen to what we deep down know is right for us, instead we listen far too much to what others think is right for us. In that way, we place ourselves in very serious situations which may lead to big torments and pain as a consequence, due to the choice we made!

It is very understandable that a lot of people pose the question why some must suffer so much – it being sad to witness a human being with so much hardship in their life. However, it is important to realize that we can not live each other's lives, neither make each other's choices and decisions, and that we surely can not take upon us the pain intended, to show the way forward to the person who is suffering.

It may become necessary to end up on the worst and most demanding way, in order to get to the essential one.
Through this walk you will be able to find the way leading you forward to a life filled with love and insight.

Illness is one of the greatest horrors that we can be put through. Suddenly we feel that our precious life is limited, either physically or mentally, and thereby we are summoned to an immediate account of our lives.
But it is by walking through the horror of your illness that you learn to reach an understanding, and to better realize the importance that lies in having the courage to say no to the external pressures that perhaps caused your illness in the first place.

Nor is it certain that we understand the purpose of our pain while we are suffering and fighting battles – but if we are able to get through it, and when the heat of the battle has cooled down, only then might we be able to understand its essential purpose as an important message.

On your walk up the stairs of life, you may have found it necessary to take a few steps backwards. Not because you had lost the ability to walk, but because you had to return to catch the steps you had skipped on your way. So once again you are able to climb the stairs of your life, only this time with firm steps and with the very top step as your target.

Let yourself constantly remember that there was not a moment in your life you could have been without, or else you would not have become the person, you are today!

∽

To escape

Escape may have many doors, and is born in the moments where we do not dare to stay where we are. It is not always easy to distinguish between escaping and just seeking solitude – however, the moments we do not stand by ourselves, and perhaps lead a conversation away from our own feelings, actions or opinions, we may very well be on the run, in order to avoid having to show our insecurities and our true self.

There are many reasons why people choose to run away from their own lives, but no matter what the reason, running away does not solve anything; rather the opposite – it might hamper expression of freedom. People suffering from some kind of addiction seldom do it because they enjoy it, but because they are trying to escape – to escape the reality of their lives. When they are sober or fully conscious, they usually become deeply unhappy about their situation, and come to realize all they have missed out on while being in their addicted state. These souls wander restless and lonely on the roads of flight, and only see life as it is, in too short moments. Because when they see their life, they are filled with pain and hurry to close their eyes, and seek refuge once more in a new drug.

The times we choose the road of escape are often because of our fear of having to be confronted with the reaction of our fellow human beings – or it may be an escape from the responsibilities we have in our daily life.

The flight may be rooted in our excuses for not taking the responsibilities life demands of us. We are not always in possession of the strength needed to confront our own feelings, instead we choose something that for a moment can take us away from what and where we do not wish to be.

We each have to take on the responsibility that follows our actions, as running away only creates yet another difficult situation, with even more mess to clean up afterwards.

Loneliness

Loneliness may be experienced as a huge and almost unbearable burden.
It may feel like a swamp in which your feet are dragging on the bottom and with your head just above the surface so that you can hear, see and breathe. Just enough to keep you alive.
You can feel so stuck in this swamp of discouragement that hope may seem to vanish. Much of what previously gave you meaning and joy, now feels as a meaningless and worthless infinity, hampering and without mercy.
It may feel like a shadow, mercilessly lowering itself over you, and grabbing you when you return home and close your door after having been out among thousands of people.

To you in this room ...
Do not let these bricks of your walls build upon your back.
Do not let yourself be burdened by these limiting ceilings. which you let sink upon you, in the despair of your thoughts.
Do not let your windows be covered with dark curtains, which shut out every sunbeam that wants to enter your mind and which furthermore steal your view of life.
Do not let your old floor-boards that are engraved with your past, splinter your feet. They may give you wounds that hurt every time you try to walk - they are trying to hamper your steps towards hope.

Get up, my dear, get up!

Grasp the opportunities of your life, catch sight of them!
You carry your freedom in your heart, so do not let it remain firmly cemented by your limiting and destructive thoughts.

Learn to appreciate what you are, and what you have, instead of striving for what you are not, and have not.

Let yourself be pleased, with the little you do, instead of feeling annoyed about all the things you did not do.

Try to be uplifted with the experiences you have on your own, instead of letting them upset you because you do not have someone to share them with.

Do not let loneliness take you prisoner and force on you a story in which you play the role of the victim. Because if you want life, it also wants you, if only you dare meet it …
Also in spite having to acknowledge that loneliness forces destructive thoughts into your mind, do not let it become master of your belief in yourself or in your own strength and will.

Do not let loneliness block the door, for you have wanted to go out for so long.
Take the first step, even if it means that you have to pass by the executioners of pain and suffering - remember, they can only cut the strings of your life if you give them permission to.

Protect yourself against these hordes of people standing on your wounded past, with eyes staring almost any belief out of you. These people are there, and you can not alter their existence.
Let go and you will no longer let their looks and opinions tie you to the totem pole of your own inferiority.

Break this curse of your life, and give into the freedom bestowed upon you by the universe. Do not let yourself be hidden away! You have been placed in this world to live your life as the human being you are.

Be open to possibilities that might appear, instead of preferring your well-known, lonely room. Say yes to thoughts from your heart, thoughts of things you for so long have felt like doing, but have not dared to do because of your fear of going out amongst others, in your fear of the unknown. Tear yourself loose! Where loneliness might grab your arms, do not let yourself give into the sights you create in your worst hour of illusion.

Try to think of your situation as it is now, and let go of thoughts of how it should have been. Remember that you are not alone, because the most faithful of all, God, embraces you, and nobody, but nobody can make him leave you, no matter what! Neither can you – as he never lets his children stand alone.

Dear you …
You have the power to break out of this enclosed room that you for so long have mourned in.
You have the strength to take the step, if you want to.

Something new must be created!
Old patterns need to be broken. Look for new experiences instead of letting yourself dwell in the quagmire of depression. Do it now! Let it no longer be postponed by excuses.

Cash your hidden cheque of possibilities, and do it at the door of freedom which will lead you back to life. Take the first step, and let life bring you what has been waiting, perhaps for a long time, for you to dare to accept it …

So even though you may still bear the invisible mark of loneliness, do not let it become your weakness, but now become your strength.

Remember that you have endured seconds, hours and long sleepless nights with loneliness by your side. You have shared a table with it when dining, at celebrations and when you have felt sorrow or desertion.

You have woken up in the morning and met its eyes first thing, in spite of the sun caressing your face with its warm light.

You are here, and you can learn from it.

The light is out there, and you carry it within you, especially on the days when darkness is at its darkest, in your longing for a twosome.

*Let loneliness be known by your heart,
but do not marry it.*

Being together in life

When a man and a woman meet in the forum of love, tones arise that create one united tune, and a beautiful melody is raised, later to be sung with the text of love in a joined song

When two human beings choose to walk down the road of life together, it is important to do so with a common goal and with love as your anchor.

That you let yourselves remember that together you have chosen each other because you want and love each other. Also on the basis of the differences you might have. The differences need not be each other's limitation, but can make up a greater strength, if you allow it.

The love between a couple will build up trust in a relationship, and vice versa, trust may build up love. This word of strength, *trust*, may take years to build, but can be destroyed in seconds.

These two ingredients, love and trust, are vital in the foundation of the couple who are on a joint journey towards the horizons of life.

So that when one feels weak, the other one steps in, to be the strength that their loved one lacks.

And where the other might feel different, space is given without questions and criticism.

Together you must assist each other's understanding that in case one of you fails, it is not because of indifference to the other, but just lacking energy – other things may for a while rob the time and attention.

You each have to try to find the joy in giving each other the freedom to choose. Do not try tying chains around the foot of your loved one, in the hope of obtaining safety and control. The more limitations, the less freedom for the joined road of pleasure and love.

It is important that both of you are able to rest safely in your hearts and minds. knowing that you are faithful to each other in your relationships with other people. No matter where you each are, you must stay faithful, in words, thought and deed.

Do not create a picture in your mind of what your loved one's action or reaction ought to be, for then you will create a gulf of disappointment when it does not turn out as you expected. Instead keep an open mind – somehow it may well exceed your expectations!
Instead, let yourself be pleased by what might come of free will. For then you know that it was done with the sincerity of joy, and because your loved one loves you.

You can give without receiving anything in return,
but you can not receive without giving.

Let yourself see the beauty that together you are able to create an oasis of flowers, and in this way build the opportunity to tie a complete bouquet, by creating a family.
Together you must help it grow in safe surroundings, and together you must share the work. No matter which winds might be blowing …
Together you must water your flowers when drought sets in, with mutual respect and a common responsibility.

Together, in well-meaning laughter, you may enjoy making fun of each other's completely unique ways of handling daily tasks. Even if they do not look like others, or the result does not turn out quite as expected. All of us are here to learn, each in our own individual way.

The trust you gradually built together must not be broken, even in the most provocative moments – as it may create distrust, shaking the trust won already.

The times where battle enters your oasis of flowers, you must try to limit the number of flowers that are trampled on. When first broken and damaged, they are rarely able to be straightened out.
So do not trample too hard where the line has to be drawn, but do it gently, respectfully and preferably with calm steps. Then you can meet up in the middle of the meadow, without having damaged each other's vulnerable flowers.

Speak with love in your tone of voice, and let the words become a message.
Then nobody has to close their ears, or shield themselves from a dangerous hurricane. Then the message will reach your loved one, without a fight, without broken flowers, or a forced grasp of soul and mind – but with a conscientious and good heart.

Love each other now, in words, thought and deed.
And live it out every day, as if it was the last one.

Reach out your hand, and embrace when the other one stumbles.
And stay an eternal support in each other's weaknesses.

Do not suffocate each other, but give each other space, so the path of life's exciting and joyous game can be played, which sometimes only can be played when you seek alone into your own soul's room.

Always speak respectfully from your heart when your loved one is talked of, no matter where or which situation you might find yourself in, that your loved one does not take part in. How do you want your love to talk about you when you are not present?

Forgive the times when misunderstanding has been
expressed in anger or misdeed.

Be present when the beautiful moments occur between you, both in experiences and togetherness.

Let your heart photograph these moments of life which only occur and appear at moments where your love has the seat of honour, and melts the two of you together. Bring out these photographs of memories at times when cold and harsh winds are causing distress in your common oasis. So that a holy place does not become a fighting arena, a fight to win with power, and which may kill all the beauty present; where the spear of comments hurts painfully and may inflict deep wounds – wounds that sometimes never heal completely.

Withdraw from this war of disputes, do not bring these fights onto the field.
You are the "adults"; you must be the clever ones, and you can also become the wise ones – if you are able to stop this fight, and instead let your minds be relieved by meeting in your common oasis, where only you two are present with no spectators expecting justice. Only God, who as a witness is pleased to watch his children return with the ball of love, that once again is able to jump to unknown heights and again play the multifarious game of life.

Now and again, make sure to meet up and call your relationship and life into account. Together, let yourselves willingly find solutions on how things might get better, and which things need to be rectified.
Then you need not be parted because of destructive accusations, but instead tie the bond between you even stronger, through your mutual freedom, respect and love for one another.

*Clouds in the sky form a smile, in the joy of
witnessing two human beings' act of love. In full bloom,
two souls travel together to unknown heights.
Coalesced and sensual, they are lifted to
the highest point, so that they together are able to touch
the unique moment of nothing.
United and in an ecstasy of love's source,
everything explodes in millions of particles. In a second
of time and with no limits.
They are, they live, and they love, in one here and now.*

Friendship

We human beings may all need some kind of friendship. Friendships may be very stimulating as we experience the world differently, and based on that, we are able to exchange our points of views.

It is so wonderful being able to share a space with the ones you have formed a friendship with, and just listen and talk.
It feels safe, and is an incredible strength to be able to be embraced by friends when we are unhappy, or when we are exposed to headwinds in our life. Because in a real friendship, we become witnesses to each other's lives, for better or worse.

Friends do not choose you because of your title or status, but because you are you.

You can not put time on a friendship as time is not determining, but the quality of its content is.

Rather have few good moments with pleasure and connectedness, than many moments of obligation.

Friends love you for what you are, and do not judge from what you ought to be.

Friendship respects the choices you might make in life, even if it means being out of contact for a while.

There is room made for an understanding of and compassion for the person you are. Not necessarily being of the same opinion, but with love and respect.

Friendship does not build on expectations, but on the mere joy of having each other. You do not consider what can be won from a friendship, but what you can add, to make it grow and become stronger in trust and mutual respect.

Friends always tell the truth,
even when it hurts.

Friends do not go behind each other's backs, in the shape of evil talk, belittlement or ridicule.

Friends stand by your side when others let you
down.

You embrace and protect the one who is your friend, regardless of others views. You stand firm, no matter where you are, or with whom you are with.

Friends always forgive where misunderstandings
have arisen.

Love in a friendship is also to set boundaries for each other as we are different – it allows you to have the freedom to say no, without being perceived as being against the other, but merely because you have a different attitude or opinion.

Friends are always faithful to you, in words, thought and deed.

When two people separate

*A wonderful sunny day went on its walk.
Enjoying the two souls, walking together
hand in hand, on the beach of togetherness.
There they wandered so beautifully and
in all their glory.
The sun rose on clime of the universe,
watching and letting its beams of light glide
across land and ocean.
As the sun in its setting turned around
and cast one last lingering glance at the day,
it sadly witnessed the two souls wander on each
side of the mountain of shadow. Sadly the sun
had to realize that a heavy and painful walk
now had begun.
The sun tried to reach out its light of hands
as help. But was rejected by the coming of night,
too late!
Darkness had already begun its walk of
its striking walking stick ...*

It is so painful having to acknowledge when we human beings are not able to steer our ship filled with mutual responsibility and love for our children and home.

It begins with tiny bumps, that play out on a troubled passage. Later on the wind picks up speed. Waves are formed on the surface and the ship is off-course; the bigger the waves, the more difficult it gets to steer.

Finally one has to loosen one's grip, and a huge imbalance arises. The ship capsizes and sinks, and inevitably everything runs out into the sea and spreads into chaos.

It may be so difficult having to break up, having to break what once seemed so safe. Suddenly being forced to divide everything into half – what, with naturally, was joined previously.

The walls of home are bare and now stand naked and empty. Once so beautifully decorated with pictures, taken in the embrace of the past, in happier times.

The framework of a home, and a flame of two candles previously burning so calmly, warm and beautifully, now becomes a sea of flames that can not be controlled, and instead burn everything to ashes.

In days to come one will witness the children's frustration over the fact that with one stroke, they must be divided in their hearts and souls. They now have to handle a new every-day life – with only one of the two, whom they previously saw and knew before as a unit.

Soft garments must catch the tears that any member of the family sheds in grief, which seem to extinguish any spark of hope.

Everything that seemed to be a strength before and represented a strong bond to keep the anchor in place, is cut in a flash, now leaving the boat restlessly, drifting around, without no direction...

Dear you ...
If you are amongst those who have reached a point where love seems to have come to an end, and your daily life together is no longer joyous, but instead has become a collision of power struggles and counteracts on each other's lives.
If you have pursued all options and to the best of your ability have tried to rescue what was, but still have come to realize that your ways must part – then you have to acknowledge in your deepest and most inner self that you have ended up limiting each other and the tone of love in your previously harmonious home.

Force yourself to stop and extinguish these fire-fights which otherwise may burn down everything to the ground in minutes, if you are not able to limit the extent of the fight.
Let yourselves meet somewhere neutral, and there speak the language of the heart as well as common sense, in honesty and mutual respect for each other's situation.

Here the possibilities might show themselves as to how to reach clarity of how you each both move on with life and soul intact.

Find it in the bottom of your heart to help each other pack and load each of your new ships that you now individually will travel in.

Try your best to draw and coordinate a chart with a schedule that makes it navigable and safe for both of you, so that you may strengthen each other's passage to each of your new harbours of life.

You must try with all your might to keep a worthy common sense and contact, so that if one of you gets off-course, the other will for a while be able to help navigate and thereby support the other's turmoil at sea.

And when your children passengers get sick or have difficulties following the new passage of life, then you again will have to meet somewhere neutral, to build lifeboats so that they will not fall overboard and drown in the upheaval in the sometimes rough sea.

Together you must do your utmost to make it as gentle and easy as possible for the children, who are part of both your lives.

For they are deeply and terribly dependent on your choices, not least in the way they came into this life!

Do not let your small children become entangled in the yarn that you yourselves might spin. See to it that you provide them with a safe and loving space where peace and love embrace them as long as the fight and struggle prevail.

Try not to burden each other with remorse or compunction. This only makes your burdens even heavier and does not promote hope for the better.

Throw your barrels of bitterness overboard so that you will be able to sail more freely and lightly. Further burdens will overload and contaminate your spirit of life on board, and thereby enter any new path which could hold back your steps in a future new life.

Do not underpin each other's ships with seaweed of lies and animosity so that your ships run aground in mud. When first they are grounded in hate and anger, they can only run in endless circles, thereby getting nowhere.

Do not throw stones of accusations at each other to justify yourself. Do not blame the other to find a guilty party in this wrong course of your common ship, because both of you are to blame!

> *Rather live happily separately*
> *than being unhappy together …*

Now it is a question of coming together in a mutual spirit, but as captains of your own individual, separate ships. Separately, you are now going to lead and create, with a new crew and a new target. Take the necessary steps to create a new and loving home, in new unknown waters of life's ocean.

Let yourselves meet one last time, before throwing your common life overboard.
Let yourselves make a joint account of your previous life together in a neutral space of reason and kindness. A sort of examination of what was, and what shall not be any more. But that has taught you and enriched your experience to manage better in the future.
You must not turn it into a discussion, but together talk as a follow-up on what went wrong. With frankness, together you must try to figure out how in the future you are to handle the children you might have.
Do not dwell on disagreements of the past, but try instead to reach an agreement which builds on the future.
It is not certain that you will be able to be reconciled in your new situation, but both of you will have learned from the past that you have created together.
Nor is it certain that you will reach an agreement, but try together to help each other to get a better understanding of what happened, and what lead you on the collision course.
Try to understand that what you have learned, may in turn become a strength in the future, so that you might become better at being two together, perhaps only with another person.
Do your heart's best to forgive each other the missteps you might both have made, as well as the times

where misunderstandings started to make their mercilessly appearances.

Try to come to the understanding that you were not against the other person, but because it was where you were emotionally at the time. Therefore you were not able to act any differently than how you did. Both of you may be deeply hurt and unhappy about what you once believed in, but which did not allow itself to be shown.

Together you have to acknowledge that you both had flaws and together you must learn to become better, but as separate individuals…

Death and sorrow

*So silent it became, all in one now disappeared, only
emptiness and nothingness fills the room that before
was home for the soul who was of this world,
but now no longer is.
Time had come for the one who departed, not to be
understood by human minds, but carefully planned
in the spirit of God ...*

So many thoughts of the mind intrude the inside questions wandering in your heart – the more thoughts there are, the deeper a pain is felt.
The fog has lowered itself heavily on the life which is left in the land of powerlessness.

- Where did you go, my dear soul?
I am sitting among thousands, but feel so alone, for it is you of all people, that I sincerely wish to be close to.

With my heart so heavy, I stop, gazing at the sky, watching the life of birds, who are on their own path, who are alive and know nothing about me standing here, getting nowhere with the loss of my dear one ...

I let my eyes rest on the calm movements of the waves, constantly in motion.

Think of all the souls, who at this moment and eternally many moments on, are on their way to God's land of heaven.
The waves do not stop, they live continuously in nature's movement as do people in the world, not knowing that my dear one no longer wanders amongst us.

Oh, dear God! Help me in this heavy hour to let go, to bid my last farewell, knowing in my heart that peace now embraces my beloved, and that you will lift up this soul.

I see the sun once more rising on the sky and over land. Beautifully, it throws its light of radiant shine that reaches anyone who let themselves be embraced by its glow so warm. I do not dare to enjoy this wonderful sight of God's fingers, bringing life and joy to all the living, as my heart seems dark, and thoughts tell me that I will lose my memory of you, if I step out of sorrow and devote myself to life in light.

I wish to wake up from my bed of grief, hoping that this departure of yours was nothing but an illusion, a dream – that I will wake up and see you near me, to hear your steps of life on my floor, and listen to your soft voice speaking. But I am sitting awake in my bed, and have to realize that you now wander in a land where living human beings can not put their feet.
People stand lovingly around me, reaching out their helping hands, wishing to show me compassion and care.

I feel their love for me and I listen to their talk from the heart.

But my heart has become silenced, and my ears have become deaf as the loss of you, my dear, who departed on your own, seems irreplaceable by loving hands or talk – only time and many tears will teach me to live the life that I have left without you.

For you, sitting there with hands so empty, in the loss and grief of your dear one.
Cry, my dear, cry! Cry for a long time if you need it – for sorrow does not know the number of days or time, but counts tears from the eyes and heart shed by you.

To forgive yourself

We become so unhappy, and it hurts so much on the inside when we have to acknowledge that we have made a mistake, and did not realize it until later.

Our innermost thoughts are usually that we want the very best for our fellow beings, and that we do not want to hurt or upset them with our actions. We often misunderstand and take it personally when we receive some kind of criticism, or when we get an answer that we did not expect. Our reaction may therefore become very intense and fierce as we are not always capable of reacting and acting rationally, according to the laws of love.

Dearest you …

You can not change past events, but you can change your behaviour, and become a loving person in your future actions. The minute you regret, you are on your way to taking important steps towards self-awareness.

You must forgive yourself – and most importantly, in the process, you must let go of the past's paralysing and eternally self-condemning thoughts, and move on from here.

Learn from your mistakes, and become better in the future.

You are not able to forget these incidents as they are stored in the memory of your heart, but you can forgive yourself for them.

Become strengthened by your past mistakes by taking the wisdom and learning you have harvested with you, so that you do not repeat the same mistake again!

Nothing can excuse or justify the actions you have made in your life, but with a deeper reflection, you may learn to become better and thereby become wiser.

Do not let your mistakes become an opponent whom you let yourself be broken down by, but a teacher, who builds you up and matures you for your future.

Love

I can make you smile and cry.
I can make anything grow.
I can light up even the darkest place.

I can be used everywhere.
Everyone is entitled to me,
and so far no one has ever had enough of me.

Through me you can achieve all the divine,
and through me you can be led out of your
distress, doubt, pain and darkness.

I am the foundation of everything beautiful
in this universe.
I am free of charge, and the quantity of me
is unlimited.
I will always be there for you,
even in case you have forgotten me.

I can heal you from your sickness
as I was created for you and to you.

You can try to avoid me and run away from me,
but no matter where you are,
I will be able to be found for you,
if you merely invite me.

The more you think and act in your deeds based on me,
the better a human being you may become, and the more

*you will love everything in this universe of God,
yourself too!*

*In that way you take part in assisting others
to benefit from me too.*

*I can create peace, harmony and order,
I am the strongest power and law in the universe.*

My name is Love …

The way to everything and the light on your walk forward.

*Through me you can seek the answers, and through me you
will find what you have been looking for.*

*Do not take me for granted,
but appreciate me when you see me.
Likewise when I am near you like an
eternal confidant in your heart.*

*Thus you will take part in
recreating a world of me.
You may begin now as you know about it,
and it therefore will be your responsibility too.*

*So therefore:
Let yourself be born in my arms,
live your life through me,
and end your days on earth
in the spirit of me.*

> *As everything you own, is nothing.*
> *but everything I embrace, is everything …*

Love is the basic ingredient of everything beautiful as it is the ultimate substance in this universe.
It is the condition of everything beautiful that might be built between a man and a woman.
It is the key pillar in happiness on their way – it builds up trust, and with its lightness, it can lift even the heaviest task.

It embraces any soul that might have fallen, it does not choose to look the other way, but stops and stretches out its hand in kindness. No matter the gender, colour, status or person.

It forgives in the moments where others make mistakes. As well as forgiving the ones who made mistakes several times!

It does not seek selfish lust, but lets itself be strengthened in the joy of contributing to others than itself.

Love may bring release to even the worst imaginable illness. And it may bring hope to the ones who have lost faith.

It does not grow thistles, envious of other people's beautiful roses, but gladly shares the joy with the happy owner of those wonderful roses.

It does not accept lies in its mouth, but shoulders any responsibility.

It does not love on condition, but always unconditionally. It makes room and reaches out to the ones returning to the light after having wandered the roads of darkness, welcomes them, provides care and shows them respect.

Instead of waiting for the next fall in the doorway of malicious delight, it always offers another chance to the one who has failed in life.

It never speaks in its own favour, but waits patiently for what it has in its heart, is clever, wise and always at the right time...

You can not elevate yourself as a loving person by means of your status or title, but only by genuine deeds from your heart, expressed in love and equal respect for other souls.

So, dear you ...
Give to the ones who might need, and forgive your fellow beings.

Love them unconditionally in words, thought and actions.

And remember that God loves you not only *sometimes*, but always, unconditionally.

Injustice

We all want to live a happy life, a life with peace on earth and in harmony with the beautiful nature that surrounds us, some close to it, others further away.
We all want to be allowed to be a part of what has been given to us, and we all need to be able to be who we are – without questions and being considered a lesser person.
But we are each individually responsible for our own actions and the way we treat other souls. Even if we meet injustice on our way ...

The feeling of injustice hits us when we feel that others violate our soul, or when we feel that those around us do not treat us with respect for what we are, and where we individually come from. Likewise, we can experience it as being deeply tragic to witness unfair treatment of our fellow human beings or animals and nature. On a large scale, this may provoke a reaction that may release contempt and rage, resulting in verbal anger, violence or other forms of powerlessness, or in the worst cases, war, with death as a consequence.

Powerlessness steps in when we get paralyzed or impotent, and feel pain and compassion for the soul being abused, or when we ourselves become subject to injustice.

It can be so painful to become witness to another's pain, having to watch their soul being violated by rejection or a lack of understanding of who they are.

If you are not able to offer your hand to them, you may react negatively, being under this heavy pressure. But it is of no help having thoughts of anger or other kinds of negative impulses as it does not release or help the person that is suffering or has suffered.

Light a candle inside of you and stand firmly in your heart's thoughts of hope and love.

Let the flame light up the darkness that might rule in human minds, and let your love embrace the one that might need it. Forgive the ones that did not know better, and ask for justice for those who are suffering.

The same applies when you yourself are exposed to an unjust treatment.

Do not seek justice in your powerlessness and disappointment, wishing that others should feel the same pain that they inflicted on you.

No matter what unpleasantness or cruelty you may be exposed to, do not let yourself forget all the uniqueness you possess in your heart, do not let struggle or doubt rule your mind, stand by the seed sowed in your heart, by you.

Forgive them, if you can, as they do not know better. Stay faithful to your heart in your words, thoughts and actions.

Only God can judge right and wrong.

Have confidence in this and embrace all human beings, even the ones not embracing you ...

Forgiveness

Forgiveness is a word often difficult to get out of one's mouth, but even more difficult it seems to offer from our hearts.

It must feel like a heavy burden for this globe that, as a planet in the universe, and a home for souls of God's seeds, through time it has witnessed human beings causing so much war, death and destruction.

This planet was the only one keeping its promise, namely to be a common home for humans, animals and nature to live in complete harmony. It was easy to fulfil until the day human beings began thinking their own thoughts…

From that very moment unfortunately, a merciless war and annihilation began, as well as a lessening of justice for the weak. A justice that later on had to be buried, as it was not allowed to receive the light of truth and love.

It was in past disagreements that forgiveness had to be content with only being a thought, and even now, it often is still just a thought; in spite of the idea of forgiveness making one of the greatest differences and being one of the most significant drivers of peace of mind in this world.

Dear you, sitting there …
Let the purest thoughts from your heart cleanse your soul. Seek into justice's chamber of wisdom to find answers.

Let yourself stop in any situation that is causing strife

which rules your life now or has ruled it before.

In your innermost thoughts, try to acknowledge your own and other people's mistakes as being actions not fully considered, but said and done in moments of fear and weakness where kindness could not get a seat.
Instead, powerlessness was given a seat in a moment's battle that perhaps was about an unresolved case that ended up as unfriendliness in the hour of pride.

Let your eyes be opened so that tears of salt water can put out the fire of anger that might rule within you.
So that it can no longer set fire to your house of love, but instead will become a valuable insight and strength in your future actions.

Rarely are there excuses for not being able to forgive another soul, only usually excuses for not getting it done.
How well do remember the moments where you hurt or offended a fellow human being with a wrong word or action yourself?

We must try to remember the times when the rope of misunderstanding have been pulled too hard by our own hands in a moment of powerlessness and later on in the aftermath, with much regret in our hearts.

To the best of our ability, we must try to reach an

understanding that when others happen to hurt us or treads on our toes by mistake, they might not have wished to hurt us, but it happened because for a moment, they allowed themselves to be carried away by fear and in their frustration defended themselves sharply with anger and words. Maybe as a protection of a past wound they carry painfully with them in their heart.

Much violence and anger could be avoided if only we were capable of understanding that we are seldom aware of the background in someone else's life when they flare up and simmer with rage, or act with contempt, defensively towards others.

We have to understand that there is almost always an emotional feeling from the past that we do not know about which can make the other person suffer painfully in their relation to others. Often when these people regain their composure, they deeply regret it and suffer intensely – knowing very well that they over-reacted in their powerlessness.
Afterwards, they have to wander alone with a burden of remorse, so that they do not dare look into the eyes of the one suffering because of their outburst.
No matter how many distractions they might seek to relieve the remorse lingering in their hearts, it will not let itself be released, until apology and forgiveness meets in the same doorway ...

I beg you from my heart to place yourself in the situation of others and yourself. Remember how all of us make mistakes during our lives – and remember too that it is first and foremost through our mistakes that we can learn to do it right in the future.

We are human beings, and we make mistakes in our relation to other people.

Many of us bring with us scars from the past, and are afraid that others will touch them.

Should a soul with self-knowledge and remorse come to your door, I ask you to:

Listen with an open heart and let him or her explain, then accept the apology they may give.

Seek no self-righteousness, but forgive, and forgive them with of all your heart.

And peace may find rest again in two now freed and released hearts ...

The art is having to acknowledge our own mistakes before being able to forgive others their mistakes.

We are only humans, and we make mistakes, and all of us make a difference, every time we whole-heartedly forgive.

To be present

Many of us find it difficult to devote ourselves to the present as we find it difficult to let go of the many thoughts passing through our brains. We are affected by what we have just come from, or perhaps are thinking of what we have planned to do next.
This causes us not to be fully and completely present in what we are really in – and therefore we are only half present.

The unforgettable moments of our life are the ones where we give into the present, and shut out everything around us, including the thoughts that might occupy our mind.
The way to be able to experience the present is to exclude the noise there might be in or around us, whether it be mentally or a physical noise.

Many humans lead busy daily lives in which daily planning is necessary, to make everything work and come together. But often when working on a task, we let our thoughts wander on to the next one before even having finished the first one! We do this because we want to be in control of what we have to take on next, and often because we believe that we get more done in this way – when actually you could say that we spend double the energy, being "two places" at the same time. When being in two places simultaneously - that is one place mentally and another physically - we divide ourselves into two.

$$\textit{Half present} \;=\; \textit{half-heartedly}$$
$$\textit{Wholly present} \;=\; \textit{whole-heartedly}$$

If we are not capable of being fully present in the now, we may risk missing out on life's important moments.

Dear you ...
It is so important for your life that you learn to become completely present in the moments that demands your attention — whether it be tangible, or when a human being needs your presence, then you will be able to give yourself fully and whole-heartedly to what you are doing.
A wonderful peace will settle in you if you are able to devote yourself completely, without disturbing thoughts. For example, when you sit in nature, totally devoting yourself to it, you will then be able to see, enjoy and sense the essentials as you will then see them with your heart.
It is by being able to be in the moment that you may experience the unique moments because they will never return - not in the same way.

The smallest moments,
might have the greatest significance ...

Which faith is the right one?

Often I am asked by people:
- Which faith or religion should I let myself be attached to?

My reply is usually:
- The faith or religion that you feel, is right for you.
And if you do not have a faith, then you should believe in love or the universe.
God does not look at which religion or faith you are tied to, but at your virtues as a human being.

All religions have the same purpose and message, namely love.

It is not a question of how often you go to church or read the Bible or words of wisdom, but in the way you act out your religion.
After all, a thief may go to church and yet go stealing afterwards!

The most pivotal thing for the sincerity of your faith will be the way you act out your love as well as how you respect and value the seed planted in you by God.

Becoming a better human being demands that from the bottom of your heart you decide to become a better human being, and hereafter act it out as well as you can, to the best of your ability.

It is only in your heart that the transformation can take place, and here the battle needs to be fought – and it is through this that you will commit yourself to what you believe in.

At my lectures and joint readings, I used to say:
- Here it is not a question of religions separating us, but of love keeping us together. If you believe, then become a better believer. And if you do not believe in anything, then become a better human being anyway.
You must remember that love always makes a difference in everything – in words, thoughts and actions.

We human beings are made of a particular substance – namely a substance only God knows, and which we call love.

It is a seed, sown in you and me, created in the name of love. A seed thriving and growing best when nurtured by what itself is made of, namely unconditional love.

Your task through life as a human being is to take care of and to nurse this seed so that:

- It will have the best growing conditions.

- When life blows its headwinds, you will shield it.

- When it has been hurt, you must help it heal again.

- If anyone tries to change it or demean it, you have to stand by it, and you must never leave it or let it down, no matter what …

That is what your task in life is about, to help, support and stand by the seed you carry in your heart. You never know which flower will develop from it!
And that is the exciting part of life – to give space, to allow all of these flowers to grow.
As to the flowers that are having difficulty growing and which may be crooked, they too must be given space and help as they are also sown by the hands of God …

Who is God?

God is the water floating in the large oceans and the water that flows in even the smallest organisms. He is the trees which stand rooted in the earth, the wind running over steppes of land, and the quiet breeze of the soft wind.

God is the night, lowering itself over land in order to be the sun that again rises in the horizon of a new day.

He is the flower which stands so beautifully dressed, he is the animals, living in nature, the lion roaring loudly when fighting for its territory. He is the bird, singing its enchanting song from its beak.
He is the new-born foal, standing vulnerable and still unsteady on its legs, but which just hours after stands and presses its muzzle into the mother's chest, hastily sucking to strengthen itself for the life to come. God is the infant, being brought into this world from its mother's womb, breathing its first breath as the first step into life.

God is Buddha, Bahaú´lla´h, Allah, Jehovah, and many others representing the all-inclusive love, in the shape of faith and the path to wisdom and spirituality in the human heart.

He is not just one, but everything and everybody.
He is for you who have a faith and even for you that have none he still is here for you.

He is the universal love, he is the pulse and life of the universe.
He is you, and he is me.
We are of God.

God is everything ...

Who can pray?

Everybody can pray because God embraces every soul who has ever been born.
He does not distinguish between colour, gender, orientation or life as we are all his precious children whom he loves always and unconditionally in his love for what is, and what will come, in his vision of the universe.

God is the eternal listener and all-embracing in his inexhaustible love. He is the light when you wander, straying into darkness – he hears your voice from the depth of your heart.

*He is the only one who is fair,
also to the unfair …*

*He forgives you, also when
you can not forgive yourself …*

He is the healing power of the disease-ridden chasm between life and you.
He builds healing bridges which may lead you to recovery when you yourself pray, and carry faith in your heart and soul.

Even at the times you may forget or run away, in your anxiety of lack of faith in life or in God, then he is always with you – he never leaves your side.

So pray, my dear, pray, and pray from your heart, for it is not important where or who you are, or which words your tongue is speaking – as it is your prayer from the heart that God embraces.

It is not important whether you know written prayers or not, but that you pray silently in your sincere heart. For God knows what worry or joy you have on your mind, and understands the lack of words in your prayer.

Before you go to sleep at night, call your day into account. Let the actions of your day see light in reflection, and empty your mind from the many thoughts taking up space. Ask your heart, in private communication with God, why you acted as you did, and what you might do differently next time to become better.

Pray for the ones you love, and pray for the ones not loving you.
Say thank you from your heart and in all humility for what has been bestowed upon you by God's hand.

Pray in your own wondrous way, say your prayer from your heart.
Pray in your belief that everything is as it shall be, as everything rests in God's hand.

Then God is pleased in his heart, as he listens to every prayer from every soul.

Regardless of words you think might be missing for a prayer, God reads the text of your heart, even before it is written. And if do you not know what praying is, then light a candle, and the universe of God will be the flame on your life's path...

༄

My prayer

*I am standing on the ground, gazing towards nothingness.
Standing on this holy planet, made of kindness,
created in wisdom, and bestowed in love.*

*Oh God! I watch your birds so free,
flying away,
raised above the oceans, carried by your winds.*

*My feet are stuck in the humanly
created existence,
furnished with lies, violence and barrenness,
a veil, attempting to cover up and deny this
beautiful truth.*

*Created in moments of fear where we human beings,
did not dare to have the courage to stand by the seed that you
planted in us.*

*I hear you calling for me, hear your voice
in my darkness.
The sound of forgiveness that I dare not believe, but
let myself be tied down with destructive thoughts,
made of confusion, doubt and fear of entering
your unknown sea of love.*

I take one step forward so that I stand naked
in your light,
exposing all my many faults and misdeeds.

Hiding my face from you, although
you have always been my witness on my path of searching
after nothingness, and love,
which I now see so clearly, is you ...

I go down on my knees and pray for your forgiveness,
in this decision of
being allowed to enter your all-embracing love,
to be given the strength and insight to walk the path that
is shown to me.
To be allowed to convey your message,
and be allowed to see with your eyes,
listen with your ears and speak your wise words.

To heal and bring your light to places ruled by darkness.
To help to understand where forgiveness
is needed.

That where violence and anger rules, I will bring
and pray for your peace.

*That where injustice rules and ruins,
I will pray for your love.
For those having lost faith,
I will bring hope into their hearts.*

*For those having gone astray and lost their way,
I will show them the way home, into the arms of your love.*

I place my life in your hands and entrust you my soul, for eternity …

www.damarislau.dk

Facebook: Damaris Lau

Instagram: Damarislauyoga

Namasté

Devotion and blessings from Damaris Lau

www.ingramcontent.com/pod-product-compliance
Lightning Source LLC
Chambersburg PA
CBHW031114080526
44587CB00011B/972